Charles Seale-Hayne Library

**University of Plymouth**

**(01752) 588 588**

LibraryandITenquiries@plymouth.ac.uk

GEOGRAPHY IN AND OUT OF SCHOOL

*Plate 1.* MAP-READING AND LANDSCAPE-SKETCHING

A party of boys map-reading and landscape-sketching on Telegraph Hill, near Midhurst, Sussex.

Fr.

# GEOGRAPHY
# IN AND OUT OF SCHOOL

*Suggestions for the Teaching of Geography
in Secondary Schools*

by

### E. W. H. Briault, M.A., Ph.D.
*Deputy Education Officer, London County Council*

and

### D. W. Shave, M.Sc., Ph.D.
*Bishop Otter Training College, Chichester*

### GEORGE G. HARRAP & CO. LTD
**LONDON    TORONTO    WELLINGTON    SYDNEY**

*First published in Great Britain* 1960
*by* GEORGE G. HARRAP & CO. LTD
182 High Holborn, London, W.C.1

*Composed in Baskerville type and printed by*
*The Garden City Press Limited*
*Letchworth, Hertfordshire*
*Made in Great Britain*

# Preface

Some of the inspiration and much of the content of the teacher's work are derived from a great variety of sources whose origins become obscure with the passage of time. The printed word, chance remarks in conversation with friends and acquaintances, formal and informal discussions, stimulus from teachers and lecturers, and the effects of new environments and experiences may all contribute to the new synthesis which every teacher makes.

The authors of this book know the truth of this and would express their gratitude to the many people, known and unknown, who have influenced their thought and helped to stimulate their ideas. They do, however, take full responsibility for suggesting the ways these concepts may be put into practice.

E. W. H. B.

D. W. S.

# Contents

# Plates

# Maps and Diagrams

# Introduction

During the last forty years geography has secured an important place in the British educational system, and to-day it is
almost universally recognized as part of the proper education of all pupils over the age of about seven years in all
types of schools. As a subject concerned with the study of
human activity in relation to the varied environments of the
world, its realism makes a strong appeal to young people.
The fact that thousands of pupils throughout the country
are being taught geography effectively is due to the knowledge and enthusiasm of teachers and to the success of the
training they themselves received in school, college, and
university. In the work of the very many successful teachers
of geography, variety of lessons and of approach is a common
factor. Such teachers will, we believe, welcome new ideas
and be glad to consider suggestions with which they are
unfamiliar about the teaching of the subject. They may also
derive satisfaction from being given advice which they already
follow. It is true on the other hand that there are many
teachers who find the subject-matter difficult to teach, some
of them because they are conscious of inadequacies in their
early training. The great breadth of the subject and the need
to condense and simplify present the teacher with very
formidable problems, yet the geography taught in school
must be the "geography of geographers," based on the facts

and using the principles and techniques of a discipline which is both scientific and humanistic.

Realizing this, some teachers have tended to use methods and to introduce principles which are more suited to maturer minds, and have found that the response of pupils, especially the slower ones, has been disappointing. The subject, in such instances, has evoked little interest, produced no tangible results, and failed to justify the time given to it on the hard-pressed timetables of to-day.

Failure to interest pupils in geography may result from a variety of causes chief among which are the wrong choice of subject-matter, the adoption of an academic approach involving too much generalizing, or the attempt to teach broad geographical principles too early. Bright pupils may be able to learn the subject easily in much the same way as the teacher learned it, but the less brilliant, the average pupils, find this approach unattractive, their learning becomes forced and uninterested, and the teaching an unrewarding labour.

The successful teaching of geography to all pupils rests on a few simple principles which can be applied in a wide variety of ways, but the breadth of the subject and the need to secure authenticity and accuracy without sacrificing simplicity make considerable demands on any teacher, the more so as geography in school, in the fullest sense of the word, is an "activity" as much as a "subject." Conferences of teachers, statements by officials of local education authorities, and comments by individuals suggest that there is a welcome desire among teachers to become aware of more effective approaches to the teaching of geography.

The chapters which follow are intended to help all those engaged in the teaching of geography to pupils over the age of ten years; they may assist the specialist as well as the class teacher who must cope with a number of subjects. While much of what is said may be helpful whatever the calibre of the pupils, the authors have had especially in mind the needs of boys and girls of average ability and those who will be following courses not leading to external examinations.

This book is intended not to be a comprehensive treatise on the teaching of geography but to emphasize certain aspects which appeal to the authors as being particularly important. Since they are convinced that the whole of the work must be based on the appreciation of the reality of the subject-matter and the awareness of the pupil as an individual, the first seven chapters consider in some detail techniques of rural and urban field-study and geography out-of-doors. Succeeding chapters deal with methods of approach in the classroom and types of syllabuses. The concluding chapters consider geography in relation to the work of the school as a whole and the implications of the subject for the pupil who will, in the near future, be a citizen of a world of shrinking boundaries and increasingly complex problems.

The book contains suggestions for the consideration of teachers which have materialized from the practical experience of two people who have been teaching the subject for many years and who have had the advantage of seeing many other people teaching it. Not all will agree with everything that is said. Teaching is an art, not a science; it is an integration of the personality, the character, the knowledge, and the outlook of each individual, and it can never be circumscribed. The best teaching methods are personal methods. Therefore the following pages propound no neo-herbartian steps, suggest no syllabuses in detail, proffer no notes of specimen lessons, provide no lists of suitable exercises, but merely make suggestions which the thoughtful teacher will modify, expand and adapt to suit his own needs.

# I

## A Sense of Reality

WE might epitomize perhaps the divergence between formal and active methods in education in the words of Teacher A, who says in effect, "I know; you learn," as contrasted with Teacher B, who says, "I will help you to find out." While in the variety of lessons which are possible, there will be a place for direct and formal teaching—and this can be done ill or extremely well—we place our emphasis unhesitatingly on the attitude of Teacher B. With Teacher A rest the dangers of authoritarianism, rewards and punishments, "learning or else," competitiveness, and, when specialist knowledge of the interesting detail is absent, the likelihood of boredom. With Teacher B rest the likelihood of that interest which is an essential in the learning process, the individual pursuit of knowledge and the pride of achievement in co-operation with others. Quite apart from the underlying character training inherent in the choice of method, the sheer effectiveness of the learning process is greatest when the sense of discovery is present; this carries with it interest, the desire to go farther, and the opportunity to express what is discovered. The expression of knowledge gained—oral, written, visual, or practical—is the confirmation of progress in learning; of this Teacher A is as well aware as Teacher B. But under Teacher B's regime, the expression will often be spontaneous and always varied, carrying on the interest aroused, and stimulating further effort.

Nearly all young children show curiosity about the things around them, in some cases a curiosity so lively as to seem a positive menace to the harassed parent. How often, particularly among average children of secondary-school age, this curiosity seems to flag, perhaps to be submerged. Can it be that a succession of Teacher A's have had something to do with it? Certainly the teacher whose attitude is, "I will help you to find out" is the one who is likely to stimulate, sustain, if necessary reawaken, that lively curiosity which is so characteristic of the exploring mind and thus of the true geographer.

In geography the sense of discovery is vital not only because it is in line with the attitude of Teacher B rather than with that of Teacher A, but because geographical knowledge springs from discovery, from exploration, from finding out real things in real places, from going and looking. In what a number of the titles of geography textbooks the word "discovery" or the word "real" figures. Geography has a natural appeal to young minds because its subject-matter is contemporary and realistic. It is not, *to begin with,* theoretical; it does not, *to begin with,* depend upon imagination or conjecture or intelligent guesswork. It can all be seen first-hand, now, in this day and age, by those people who have eyes to see and understanding to bring to the consideration of their own surroundings. Geography describes the earth. It may do more: analyse, synthesize, interpret; observe correlations and evaluate causal relationships; but *first* it depends on going and looking. It culminates in the art of description, albeit description of an interpretative and qualitative kind, and description invariably graphic as well as verbal.

The going and looking is as realistic as school dinner, and may be a good deal more interesting. This sense of reality must always infuse our geography teaching. We must always have in mind the sense of exploration, the fact that whatever we may say or the book may describe has sprung from the observation of those who set foot upon the land. We must also always see as our goal a geographical description which is so realistic that the area described comes alive in the mind and is as vivid in the imagination as if it were the living environment outside the school; and at the same time so well-informed and well-considered, through the processes of scientific analysis of data and intelligent appreciation of relationships, as to present a picture which is not only realistic but accurately interpretative.

Between the original exploration and the final description lie the pitfalls; and it is when the primary emphasis is laid upon the steps between that an academic type of work results, capable of assimilation by the minority but unrealistic and therefore uninteresting to the average pupil. It is not to be supposed that we advocate the omission of the steps between, even with less able pupils; but we suggest that it is not through theoretical generalizations or the academic dissection and analysis of factors that the study of an area is best initiated. Rather we should have so clearly in mind the vital importance of a sense of reality that we approach the study of an area as if we were exploring it ourselves, and move on to the analysis and examination of relationships only when we have fully established the feeling that we are dissecting what we know, as if at first hand, to exist. That being said, let us add that even the dull pupil is capable of recognizing correlations between geographical facts, of appreciating realistically that man lives his life differently in different parts of the world because of the differences of his environment.

How are we to achieve this permeation of the sense of reality even into those parts of our geography which are more theoretical, more generalized, or more analytical? Ordinarily we suggest by going from the particular to the general. This principle of approach applies at two levels: at the level of the whole scheme of work and at the level of the pattern of a single lesson, or a few lessons devoted to one particular study. At the level of the scheme of work we shall try to build up a realistic appreciation of different environments by beginning with the local and not approaching the very strange too quickly; and we shall defer sweeping generalizations and world patterns until they can be based upon a reasonable amount of realistic knowledge. At the level of the week-by-week work we shall go from the farm to the prairie, from the mine to the mining area, from the large-scale map to the atlas, from the weather to the climate, and not vice versa.

Consider the unreality, *as a first approach,* of a map of the wheat-growing areas of Canada: a map of North America a few inches across with a shaded area whose northern curved boundary has some magical significance to be drawn and remembered. Contrast, *as a first approach,* an air photograph of the prairie landscape, an oblique on which the farmstead can be seen: some one's home, some one's work and livelihood; and from that to the interminable miles and the limit beyond which the plough does not reach.[1]

Consider, *as a first approach,* the outline-map of Britain: "Now we will begin by marking in the coalfields"—those black and meaningless blobs which are to be numbered and named, perhaps by southerners who have never seen a winding gear in their lives. Contrast the powerfulness of a vivid description of the sickening drop of the cage down the shaft, the well-illustrated résumé of how the coal is gained and raised, the naming and location of a particular mining town; and *then* the mention of the areas where this is men's way of life.

Consider the realism of a description of the May heat in Bombay, such that an egg smashed on the pavement will cook in a trice, or of the January cold in Tomsk, such that water poured from a cup will freeze before it reaches the

[1] This approach is developed in Chapter 10, p. 113.

ground. How much more effective as an introduction than turning to the isotherms on page so-and-so or learning about the pressure belts which explain the monsoons. Not that the isotherms or the pressure belts are to be for ever neglected, but that the conditions they summarize or explain must first be made realistic to the pupils whatever their ability.

Better than these devices and even more successful than these strategies of approach, of course, is geography at first hand. The sense of the reality of that which cannot be experienced will be much more likely to be achieved if the pupils have had personal experience of the geography all around them. The feeling of exploration will be more present in the geography-room if from time to time the pupils go out and discover some geography for themselves. It is important that some, at least, of this out-of-doors geography should be done by the class as a whole with the teacher; for through it common standards in the understanding of geographical terms can be built up. A hill or a mountain, a steep slope or an undulating plain, mean different things to different pupils even in the same class until their geographical experience in common has been enlarged with the guidance of the teacher. But much of this vital, first-hand geography can be carried out individually or in groups, and in such ways the exploratory sense may be keenly developed. Even when the class is together the teacher will be wise to avoid making the occasion one for too much direct instruction, and to lay the emphasis upon pupil activity.

Let us, then, seek to achieve a sense of reality in the minds of our pupils in all their geographical work, through work which is direct and real, and through ways of learning which are large-scale and realistic in their approach to distant areas and to generalizations and causes which are necessarily more theoretical. We may suitably begin by considering the application of this principle to the countryside, especially in the sense of the cultivated land, of our own country.

# 2

## The Land

MOST of the boys and girls of this land of ours live in towns, many of them in cities or sprawling conurbations which have pushed back the untouched countryside beyond walking distance. Only a small minority of our boys and girls live in sufficiently close contact with the land to appreciate directly the attitude of the farmer towards it, the part it plays in the mind and make-up of the true countryman. Yet upon the land we all depend. To our boys and girls cereals come in cardboard boxes, roots may be seen when bulbs are grown in glass jars, seeds are obtained in packets, fruit arrives in crates and is displayed on barrows, milk comes in bottles, and meat is red and white and tied with string or skewered. It is true that from an early age a relationship between corn and cornflakes, between orchards and apples, between cows and milk is inculcated and appreciated; but such appreciation does not readily extend to an appreciation of the land, the very soil upon which these products depend. Even we, the urban teachers, though we carry our minds beyond the corn to the labour of harvest, beyond the cow to the cud, from the orchard to the insecticide or the frost protection, do not always understand the land itself, could not always tell a good field from a poor one, and do not all of us really know what the farmer means when he speaks of the land being in "good heart."

Yet without the land, without the yearly round of seedtime and harvest, ploughing and reaping, all our technical skill, all our mechanical civilization, would be as ashes to an empty belly. Whatever else we may do, we must eat, and from the soil of this land and others springs directly or indirectly almost every scrap of nourishment we receive. This deep, permanent, and primeval significance of the land is something of which the town child is profoundly unaware. Yet surely it is something quite fundamental in the education of every single person. From time to time we are told by eminent persons, some educationists, some not, what are the minimum requirements of an educated person—an appreciation of the literary and artistic culture of the civilization in which he lives; an awareness of the history which lies behind the pattern of contemporary society; an understanding of the "scientific outlook." Among the sometimes formidable list is frequently, and rightly, some understanding of the environment, the homeland and the world in which he is set to live his life, a claim for the importance of geographical knowledge which, as has been said, is now widely accepted. It is our present suggestion that a vital part of this universally needed geographical understanding is a realistic awareness of man's dependence upon the soil.

In accordance with our principle of proceeding from the particular towards the general we suggest that the development of this awareness should begin along two parallel lines —namely, through a farm and through a year. This is something which may be, but may not have been, done at quite an early age; but whether or not the child may have had this experience at seven or eight years of age, it is desirable that it should be gained or repeated early in the secondary course when it may be a fuller one and set against a wider background of knowledge and experience. Let us introduce our pupils to one or two particular farms, if possible at first hand; if this cannot be arranged, then with large-scale maps, pictures, and as many details of crops and stock as possible.

Then let us also follow the farmer's year, season by season, appreciating as far as possible the importance of weather changes and the influence of these daily factors of common experience upon his work, and his success or failure with this or that crop or livestock. We must be prepared to find out about ploughs and harrows, drills and rollers, reapers and binders, harvesters and balers. The use of fertilizers and the importance of crop rotations emphasize the value of the soil itself and the need to keep it in good heart; the relationship between crops, stock, and manure, so commonplace to the farmer, is something which has to be learned and understood by the town child. One of the best ways, aside from first-hand experience, in which this work may be done is through "Farm Adoption," the scheme organized by the Association of Agriculture.[1] For a small fee each adopting school receives full particulars of a farm and regular letters regarding the work upon it.

Following the farm and the farming year, we may attempt to get our pupils to appreciate the variations in the land within this small country of ours, looking at them, not as old rocks and new rocks, or hilly lands and flat lands, but as the farmer would look at them. It may be best to do this by extending the idea of farm study to farms dissimilar to the mixed farm we have presumed as our first example. The hill farm with its steep and rocky grazing and its few stone-walled fields and hardly won crops will form one illustration. As a contrast the marsh farm, chosen to illustrate the quality of rich pasture, where drainage is a major problem, or the fen farm, where the deep, dark, rich soil yields good crops but water is still the enemy, may be studied. What kind of land produces our orchard fruit and our potatoes? This is the sort of question that should arise and be answered as realistically as possible.

Perhaps at a later stage we shall seek to give our pupils

[1] The Association of Agriculture, 53 Victoria Street, London, S.W.1

an awareness of the striking differences between the farmer's land in different parts of the world. They should come to recognize that the intensively cultivated, mixed farming land of Western Europe is not characteristic of the greater part of the earth's surface; that the farmer producing "money" crops has a very different outlook from that of the primitive cultivator whose yields are mainly for subsistence. We may seek to show what the "land" means to the peasant of India and south-east Asia: a small plot, a flooded garden of a farm. We may compare the Mediterranean *huerta*, the sun-drenched and irrigated garden set in a pocket surrounded by the sun-burnt dust and stones where the goats are driven. We should try to bring alive the land of the prairie farmer, the thin black soil, the uniformity, the sparsely spaced wheat, the rhythm of the year, with its idle winter and few summer months of furious activity so different from the rhythms of the English countryside. These and other important and typical food-giving environments are all part of the picture of the soil, so many different varieties of which help to sustain life in this industrial land of ours.

Another important aspect of the significance of the land which these studies should inevitably bring out is the possibility of the misuse as well as the good use of the soil. Our homeland farms will have shown the care needed to balance the soil budget so that the land remains in good heart. What are the other kinds of lands in which the budget is balanced equally well but in a different way? What of the lands where extensive farming amounts to soil mining? Soil erosion, whether of the dust bowl or the water-erosion of the one-time forest lands, is a dramatic subject, well-documented and readily presented to pupils through film and picture. The figures alone can be dramatic—the Mississippi dumps 400 million tons of mud into the Gulf of Mexico every year; from the farm lands of the United States the annual loss of soil is enough to fill a freight train which would encircle the earth eighteen times. The answer to all this is also striking, and raises issues of economic and social significance which older pupils will recognize and discuss.

What of the alienation of farm lands to other purposes, particularly in a small country such as ours already heavily dependent on other lands for her food? The Scott Report[1] estimated that in the twelve years 1927-39, 794,000 acres (over 1200 square miles) of good agricultural land had been taken for urban development, aerodromes, playing fields, etc., and the trend has continued during and since the War. Some use will be made of the Land Utilization Survey maps[2] and some attention given to the planning controls and the opposing interests around our great cities, in respect of the still open land. The siting of new towns is worth consideration, the kinds of needs of suburban building, of factory development, of "amenities," and the continual loss of farm land, often fine market-garden land, to other interests, should call for investigation, report, and discussion. For those who teach country children much of this background may be taken for granted. Usually, however, the striking differences between farming in one part of the country and another will need to be realistically established; and indeed it has to be remembered that what is familiar to the average pupil is not always properly understood.

While the importance of the land and the soil as the source of food and life is fundamental, two related matters may be mentioned. First, it is in studies of the kind we have described, particularly if carried out in the field but also if made only in the geography-room, that the wholeness of knowledge is so evident, and that the synthetic character of the geographical study is so apparent. It is the essence of

[1] *Report of the Committee on Land Utilization in Rural Areas* (H.M.S.O., 1942). See also *The Land of Britain: Its Use and Misuse,* L. D. Stamp (Longmans, Green, 1950).
[2] The data for these were collected before the Second World War.

geographical study, first to analyse, then to draw the picture in the round. In a farm study the synthesis is almost forced upon the attention, the relationship between nature and man to an extent obvious. How does a farmer or a land-agent recognize good-quality land? How can he tell a clay or a sand or a limestone soil? The answer is frequently by its plants. Where chickweed grows crops will grow well; where the buttercup is there is clay, and so on. Certain trees are well known as indicators of soils. In other words, in looking at the land we need to be naturalists as well as geographers; and in understanding many of the social and economic features we cannot afford to neglect history as well.

Secondly, we may consider the importance of the country-side to the town-dweller. The open-air and the country, the hill-walk and the river are a great refreshment to those whose lives are set in streets and factories. The English countryside is part of our natural and cultural heritage which young people need to be taught to appreciate and to preserve. The alarming increase of litter in this pleasant land of ours is something which we teachers must expect to do our share in preventing. If we, the town-dwellers, are to continue to be allowed to follow footpaths and tracks, then our under-standing of the farmer's work must be at least sufficient to ensure that we do not break down fences or leave gates open. Some training in country manners like training in ordinary courtesy should probably form part of our jobs as teachers. And who better than the geography teacher? For none but he is likely to teach or perhaps to understand fully the significance of the land.

# 3

## A Day in the Country

WE regard direct geographical experience of the countryside as of the utmost importance, especially for town
children. We do so because through it the sense of reality,
the exploratory spirit, are best of all realized, and because
it is vital for pupils to appreciate the significance of the land
itself. To give children direct experience of the countryside is
a matter of time, money, and organization; to give them
geographical experience requires knowledge, understanding,
and careful planning on the part of the teacher. What constitutes geographical experience of the countryside? Briefly,
that kind of experience which gives a boy or girl "an eye for
country"—that is to say, some degree of ability to look at
the landscape interpretatively. It involves some understanding
of the physical basis of land forms, at any rate of the more
straightforward kind, and sufficient understanding of the
human activities of the countryside to be able to recognize
relationships between them and the natural environment in
which they are to be seen. Let it not be thought that this kind
of understanding is the prerogative of the able pupil. Often
out-of-door experience is the means of awakening interest on
the part of the less bookish pupil who responds quickly to the
realities of the open-air situation.

This "eye for country" is something which, once initiated,
is readily improved and deepened by experience with the help
of background reading. If a geography teacher should feel

that he does not possess it even sufficiently really to understand what is meant by the phrase, then let him forthwith
take steps to be in the countryside with an experienced field
geographer, who can start him on something, the interest and
pleasure of which he will quickly find increases with each
further step of understanding he takes. The best way of
arranging such experience is through the Geographical Association's[1] Summer School or Spring Conference or through
a teachers' course at one of the centres of the Field Studies
Council.[2] For the school pupil an eye for country is to be
developed gradually through interesting and active experience, followed by suitable follow-up work in the classroom.
The first two vital steps are readily taken through experience in almost any area. They are, first, to recognize and
be convinced that the shape of the land is determined by
physical processes—weathering, erosion, deposition; secondly,
to realize actively that plants (whether crops or trees or wild
plants) grow on the *land*, and have a relationship, whether
of simple cause and effect or not, to the physical landscape.
These two are really the key to further investigation and
study. Other important realizations, such as that people have
built farms or houses in particular places very often for good
reasons, may come a little later.

We suggest that the underlying objective we shall have
in mind in taking our pupils into the countryside will be
understanding rather than simply factual knowledge. Nevertheless, this field experience will in fact extend our pupils'
knowledge and will impress upon their minds the identity of
many things which they may have seen pictured and read
about but which they have never touched or seen "in the
round." A field of wheat, a herd of cows, a meandering
stream and a flood-plain; these commonplace things and
many others may be quite strange as first-hand experiences to

[1] C/o The Branch Park Library, Duke Street, Sheffield, 2.
[2] 9 Devereux Court, London, W.C.2.

some of our town children; or if not strange yet not necessarily confidently recognized or linked up with what may
have been seen and heard in the geography-room. We have
already mentioned the value of direct geographical experience
in common and with the geography teacher, in ensuring a
common standard of acceptance of the meaning of the
simpler geographical terms. Another important factor is the
psychological value of seeing physical processes in the landscape actually at work: a stream wearing away its banks,
the waves moving shingle on a beach, the loose surface of a
steep slope without a continuous vegetation cover. For pupils
familiar with country ways this experience in the realm of
physical geography is still important. (For them, of course,
urban study would be novel and significant.) The conviction
of a few examples actually experienced is likely to be carried
over into related spheres where the boy or girl must rely
upon the teacher or the textbook for the description or
explanation.

There are various ways of arranging geographical experience in the countryside for children. Some may be taken on
school journeys for a week or a fortnight, and in this way
introduced to the countryside and the seashore as well as to
related interests such as those of an historical character,
under the guidance of teachers able to identify and explain.
Similarly boys and girls may spend, say, a fortnight at a
school camp, perhaps one of the camps formerly run by the
National Camps Corporation and now in many cases by the
local education authority. Here both they and their teachers
will find educational facilities and help which they are
unlikely to get on a school journey. Whether or not our pupils
have the benefit of experience of this kind, we should regard
a day in the country at least once a year as an essential part
of the good geography course. On school journeys and from
school camps there will be days in the country too, and we
propose therefore to consider ways in which such occasions

may be best planned and organized, in order to get the utmost out of what may be time hardly wrung from our other specialist colleagues for this whole day out of school.

We cannot emphasize too strongly how important it is for the teacher to be thoroughly familiar with the ground to be covered and to plan carefully the details of the day. Nothing is more miserable or more profitless than the day in the country in which the teacher tries to lead along a route he does not know, through country of which he is ignorant, a group of children who are being given nothing to do but walk. We must be sure of our route, we must be familiar with our countryside and have a good understanding of it, and we must plan in detail what the children are to be doing during the day as well as walk. We shall elaborate the last point shortly. Before doing so, let us consider the day in the country as part and only part of a unit of geographical work. The day will be preceded by preparation at school. This should be of two kinds : straightforward practical preparation of what is needed to carry out the actual work in the field, and background preparation of general principles which may be especially important in relation to the examples we shall meet in the field. We think it undesirable to attempt to describe to the pupils in advance all the things we shall hope to see during the day. This hinders rather than helps the learning process, for it diminishes the element of surprise and wonder, and the opportunities for "discovery," and hampers the creation of the exploratory spirit. But it may be necessary to explain a few general processes so that specific examples can be discovered and seen to illustrate or to be a part of a general pattern. (A good example would be some preparation on the work of rivers in advance of a day when a good river cliff was to be seen.) It may be desirable to indicate with the appropriate large-scale maps the route to be followed. Sometimes, perhaps, an attempt will be made to imagine what the landscape will look like in relation to a particular part of the map; but we feel that this should be done only occasionally. The practical preparation needed will relate to the work to be done, and its nature will become evident as we consider the day's programme. We shall not attempt, therefore, to describe it by itself.

The teacher is prepared, the class briefed. How, then, shall we plan our day? Some remarks on purely practical points may not be out of place. On many occasions at any rate our first problem will be one of transport. There are many advantages in a privately hired coach, especially that it gives flexibility to the pattern of the rest of the day. A coach can pick up the class at the school itself. (Let it be emphasized in passing that we strongly advocate taking a whole class and not a mixed or selected group, for the advantages of a geographical experience *in common* accrue most fully when the unit is the class.) A coach can not only set us down at a point where it is really convenient to start walking but can pick us up at the end of the day at quite another and equally convenient point. There is often a gain also in using the coach for a stage in the middle of the day. Such an arrangement means that lunches need not be carried round, that changeable weather conditions may be more readily coped with; and that there is a perhaps welcome break from walking during the day. A dull stretch of road between two more interesting points of the route may very suitably be covered by coach if one is used. On other occasions the railway will serve our purpose. Public buses are generally to be avoided if our numbers are those of a whole class. Other practical points to be covered by previous planning are a suitable lunchtime spot where toilet arrangements can be made and drinks obtained—without the promise of the latter some children will always be found to load themselves with bottles of "pop"—and again an opportunity for liquid refreshment before the return journey. Some advice to pupils on footwear and clothing is also a wise precaution.

It is to be hoped that the day in the country as an essential part of the year's programme in geography will not be precluded by shortage of funds. Many local authorities make a capitation grant to cover out-of-school visits of all kinds. The geographer's laboratory is out-of-doors and expenditure on transport should be regarded in the same light as expenditure on chemicals in the science laboratory or upon paint in the art-room. Many schools supplement whatever may be allowed officially by drawing on a school fund built up—who knows how?—and designed to provide these little extra amenities for games and school matches, for out-of-school activities, and for visits of various kinds. We geographers ask for no more than our share; but our request is based upon a conception of our subject and its teaching, in which countryside experience is an essential and not a frill.

The key to a successful and happy day-excursion lies in the busy-ness of the pupils. If the pupils are unaccustomed to walking they must forget their physical exertions in the succession of interesting things they have to do, to find out, to collect, and so on. From the teacher's point of view the preliminary planning already mentioned as so essential should aim at ensuring this active succession. It will include a certain number of stops when the teacher talks to his pupils, pointing out, identifying, explaining, asking questions. There should not be too many of these stops; they should be at carefully selected places, and the amount of talking should be a minute or two only in each case. Children will not listen overlong in a countryside probably full of interest. In any case talking in the open air to thirty children is hard on the voice. In planning the stopping places it is worth while taking trouble to make sure that the teaching point in each case is made from the most suitable and striking viewpoint. It is no good stopping the class in order to say to them, "Now, if those trees were not in the way you would be able to see . . . . . , so look out for it as we go on." They won't.

The use of a large-scale map is of great value. We shall need at least one map between two pupils. As well as generally encouraging the pupils to follow the route on their maps, it is wise to arrange a few specific map-reading stops and a few items of discovery to be made in relation to the map. "What is the building shown by the rectangle at . . . . . . (*grid reference*)?" "How high is the very steep slope shown by the black cliff marking at . . . . . ?" "Find out from the map the name of the highest hill to be seen from . . . . . ." One of the most valuable techniques involving map-reading and observation is the landscape sketch. This should be a simple line drawing of the main outlines of a view with the chief features named (Figure 1). The steps in such a piece of work, which is certainly not beyond those of average ability, seem to be three : first, to relate the view to the map and to identify outstanding points and places from the map (see Plate I); second, to sketch the outlines; third, to return to the map and with its help to name on the sketch those points identified to begin with. The second task, of course, requires practice and calls for help from the teacher. The commonest fault, and one from which, in our experience, teachers themselves are not always free, is to draw slopes at steeper angles than is really the case. The pencil held up with the arm extended will help to check and correct this. Good landscape sketches have a great value when later in the classroom we carry out the vital follow-up work which really establishes geographical points in the pupils' minds.

Another group of jobs to be done on the day-excursion comes under the general heading of "finding out." It is most valuable to give practical experience not only of map-use but of the limitations of the map as a source of geographical information. We shall ask our pupils to find out in the field facts and explanations which they could not discover except by going and looking, and in the process teach a fundamental lesson. Consider how many significant geographical facts are

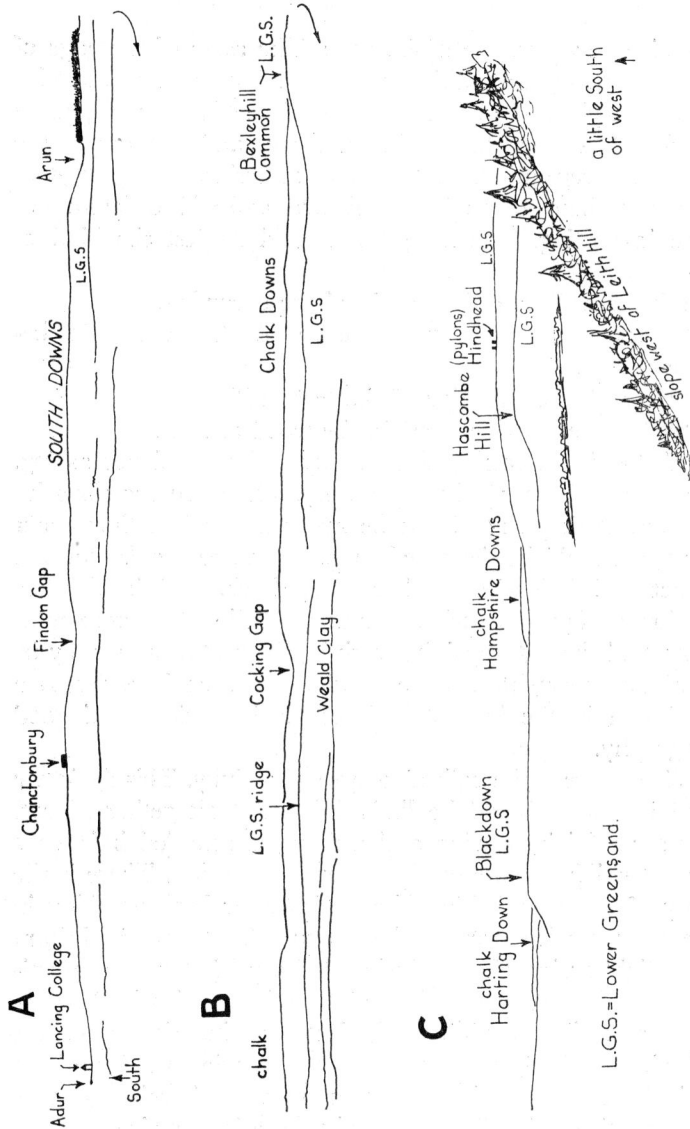

Fig. 1. Panorama Sketch from Leith Hill, Surrey

In the whole sketch the right-hand end of A would join to B, and the right-hand end of B to C.

not given even on the 2½-in. map. The slope of the edge of
a river terrace, the position of the break of slope at the edge
of a flood-plain, the nature of the surface of a steep slope, the
height of a river bank, the land-use, and the crops, the
dominant vegetation, the building materials in a village or
farm : all these our pupils can discover and add to the map or
note in writing. The list given should suggest the kind of
question we should ask, and the teacher will readily add to
the list according to the terrain of the excursion.

"Mark on your map the edge of the flood-plain between . . . . . ."

"How high is the edge of the terrace?"

"What are the chief trees in the wood at . . . . . ?"

We tend to stress finding out by looking and not asking.
The former is genuinely exploratory. There are occasions for
asking but they should not be many, and when they occur
the task should be delegated to two or three pupils who are
to act on behalf of all and to report back. Additional information on farming such as numbers of livestock, crop rotations, and the nature of the work in different seasons, may be
legitimately sought, but we should keep such inquiries to a
minimum in the interest both of good relations and good
geography.

Then there is the collecting type of activity. This again we
would suggest should be limited but not altogether absent.
Some careful instruction and training are needed before we
can let children loose on the natural vegetation. There is the
story of the householder who could never keep anything in
the front garden because the treasure hunt organized from
the neighbouring H.Q. (of who shall say what Youth organization?) always began with the instruction, "Bring back something green." Nevertheless, children may be asked to collect
*a* leaf from the dominant tree in a particular wood, perhaps
a single ear of corn, better two or three small rock specimens
from particular localities, a rolled pebble from a river terrace,

sometimes certain specified wild flowers or wild fruits. Whatever may be collected, location is most important, and we should stress the need for the pupil to record with the help of his map where the find has been made. The choice of the items must be carefully made so that no damage is done in the countryside and so that what is collected is not too cumbersome to be brought back to school.

The various types of activities will of course be mixed up together and provide a varied succession. The example which follows is from an area often visited by children from Greater London, and the questions have proved in practice interesting to, and readily within the scope of, children of quite moderate ability (Figure 2).

As part of our preparation at school for the excursion we shall either provide the list of questions on a duplicated sheet or see that the questions are entered up in a notebook ready. In either case it is important to ensure that the pupils are prepared to make a suitable record of what they see and find out as the day progresses. A small field notebook which will go in the pocket is desirable.

The kind of day in the country which this sort of technique will provide is not the only way in which children can do geographical work in the countryside; some further techniques of study are described in the succeeding chapter. Nevertheless, it is a profitable and natural technique, in that it is really a carefully organized version of what any good geographer does by second nature when on a country walk, and of what, in some measure, we may hope our pupils will come to do on their own account as they develop an eye for country. The geographer when walking invariably map-reads, often sketches, certainly finds out and interprets, and frequently collects. Along with the process of geographical education which is our main objective during a day such as this there can and should be at least two further educational opportunities which the teacher will seize. First, he will take the opportunity of training

## MOLE GAP, BOX HILL
(Follow your route on your map all the time)

1. Is the railway straight?
2. Is the cut-off meander natural or artificial?
3. How can you tell that the flood-plain is sometimes flooded?
4. Which way is the River Mole flowing?
5. What are the main trees of the flood-plain?
6. What flowers grow in the wood?
7. How is Ham Bank formed? Draw it.
8. What is at the top of Ham Bank?
9. What is a swallow-hole?
10. Write a note on Lodge Farm.
11. What happens to the river here?
12. Compare Swanworth Farm with Lodge Farm.
13. From Norbury Park look back and sketch the Mole gap.
14. What are the main trees of the chalk?
15. What happens to the railway and why?
16. What is the shape of the Norbury Park spur?

(Lunch!)

17. Where is the village of Mickleham sited?
18. What building materials are common?
19. Write a note on the constable's swallow-hole.
20. What materials are used in the church?
21. Compare the chalk woods with the vegetation on the clay with flints. Can you tell when you walk on to the clay?
22. From White Hill, find Juniper Bottom, Lodge Hill, and Ranmore Church. Where is the Mole?
23. The Headley valley is parallel to the chalk scarp. What is its section like?
24. Juniper Bottom is at right angles to the chalk scarp. What is its section like?
25. From Lodge Hill, find Headley Church.
26. What are the plantations on Lodge Hill?
27. What can you see from Box Hill?
28. What is the Box Hill river cliff ("The Whites") like?
29. How has man made use of the Mole gap?
30. What does "The Whites" look like from Burford Bridge?

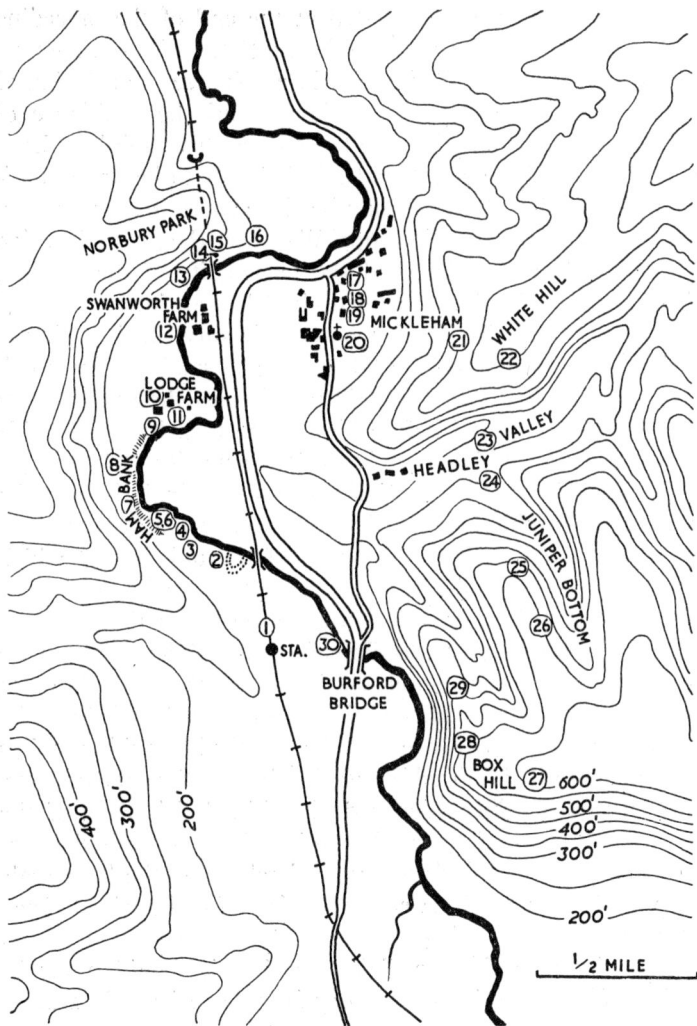

Fig. 2. MOLE GAP, BOX HILL

boys and girls, as was suggested at the end of the preceding chapter, to respect the countryside and to treat it well. He may refer to the Country Code; he will emphasize the shutting of gates, respect for crops and animals, and the avoidance of litter. Second, he may be able to heighten his pupils' aesthetic appreciation of the countryside. This is not to be done pontifically or sentimentally; it may be done more in conversation with individuals or small groups. Whatever the method, which will depend on the class and the personality of the teacher, there is no doubt that the town child has an innate sense of wonder and admiration for natural beauty. It is rather a thrilling reward for trouble taken to see a small Cockney lad, on emerging from the Box Hill woods into the open, where the Weald lies spread before him, come to a halt with wide eyes, and to hear him remark, in deep sincerity, "Cor!"

So much for the day itself, the second and main item in the unit of geographical work of which preparation in the classroom was the first. The third part of the unit is that which establishes the educative value of the rest—namely, the followup at school. It is of great importance to go over the excursion with the class as soon as possible afterwards. The maps will be given out again, each pupil will have his record for the day; and we shall trace in imagination the geography of the walk. Questions set in advance will be checked, teaching points brought home with blackboard sketch, question and answer, and any outstanding queries dealt with. A fair copy of the record may be usefully made, and perhaps a small show of notes, sketches and finds set out and related to the large-scale map used. This can be a rewarding item for the school Open Day or parents' evening (Figure 3). The follow-up need not last too long nor be too elaborate; but it should never be omitted if the day in the country is to have its full value.

The Bridge Shoreham.

VIEW FROM VALLEY SIDE ABOVE STATION

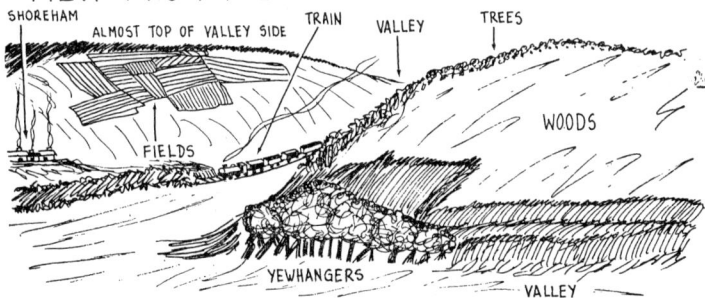

SHOREHAM
ALMOST TOP OF VALLEY SIDE
TRAIN
VALLEY
TREES
FIELDS
WOODS
YEWHANGERS
VALLEY

View of the Valley showing the scarp and dip slope

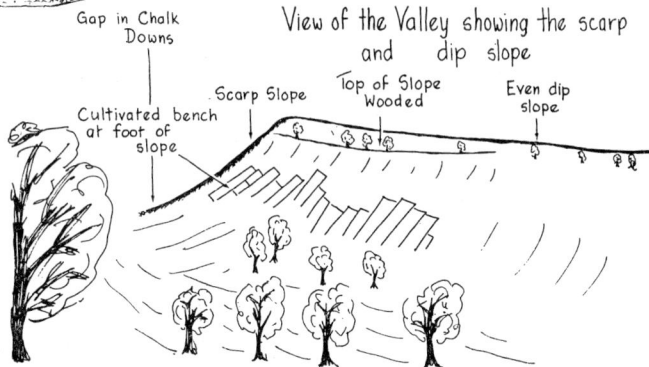

Gap in Chalk Downs
Scarp Slope
Top of Slope Wooded
Even dip slope
Cultivated bench at foot of slope

Fig. 3. THE OPEN DAY EXHIBITION

On this and the two following pages are reproduced some of the actual work done by pupils in the field, which formed part (but only part) of the exhibition of field-work.

# TRANSECT FIELDSHEET

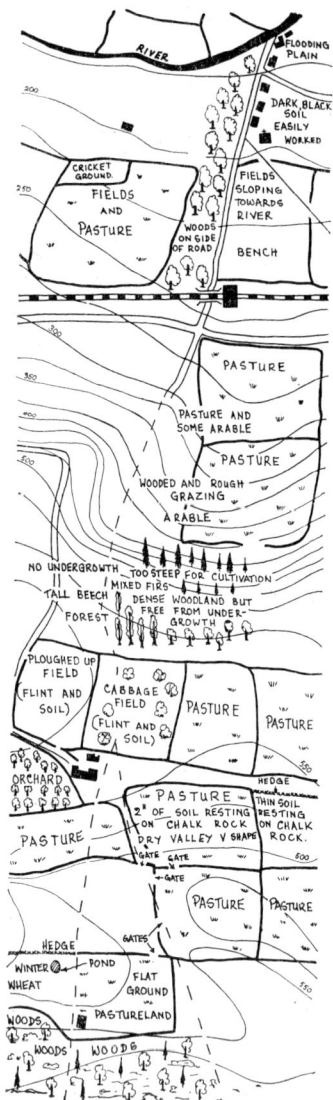

RIVER

FLOODING PLAIN

200

DARK BLACK SOIL EASILY WORKED

CRICKET GROUND

250

FIELDS AND PASTURE

FIELDS SLOPING TOWARDS RIVER

WOODS ON SIDE OF ROAD

BENCH

300

PASTURE

350

PASTURE AND SOME ARABLE

400

PASTURE

450

WOODED AND ROUGH GRAZING

ARABLE

NO UNDERGROWTH

TOO STEEP FOR CULTIVATION

MIXED FIRS

TALL BEECH FOREST

DENSE WOODLAND BUT FREE FROM UNDER-GROWTH

PLOUGHED UP FIELD

(FLINT AND SOIL)

CABBAGE FIELD

(FLINT AND SOIL)

PASTURE

PASTURE

HEDGE

ORCHARD

PASTURE

2" OF SOIL RESTING ON CHALK ROCK DRY VALLEY V SHAPE

THIN SOIL RESTING ON CHALK ROCK.

PASTURE

GATE GATE

GATE

500

PASTURE

PASTURE

HEDGE

GATES

WINTER WHEAT

POND

FLAT GROUND

550

WOODS

PASTURELAND

WOODS

WOODS

WOODS

THE OPEN DAY EXHIBITION (*continued*)

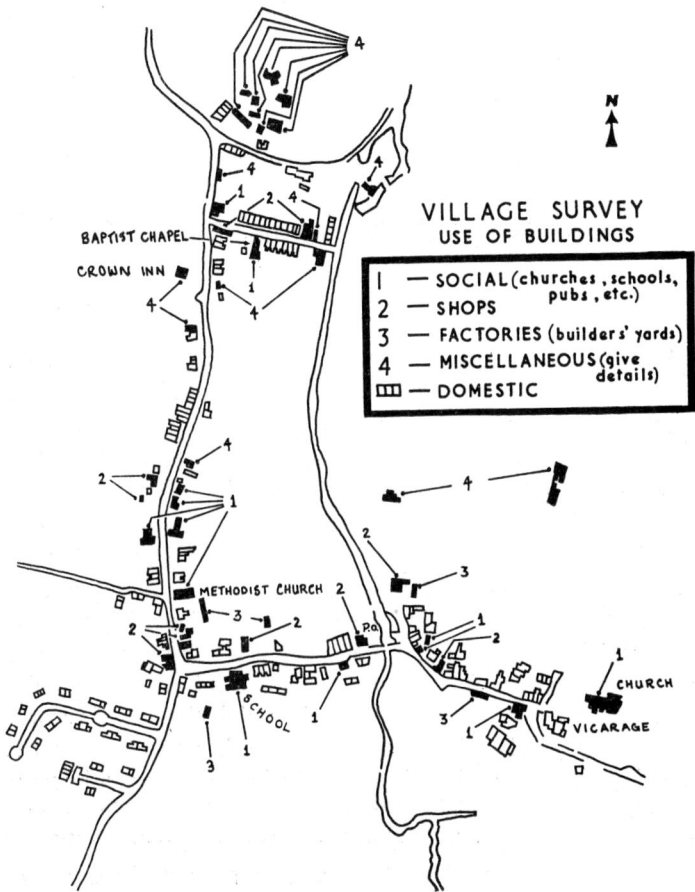

### VILLAGE SURVEY
#### USE OF BUILDINGS

| | |
|---|---|
| 1 | — SOCIAL (churches, schools, pubs, etc.) |
| 2 | — SHOPS |
| 3 | — FACTORIES (builders' yards) |
| 4 | — MISCELLANEOUS (give details) |
| ▥ | — DOMESTIC |

BAPTIST CHAPEL

CROWN INN

METHODIST CHURCH

SCHOOL

CHURCH

VICARAGE

THE OPEN DAY EXHIBITION (*continued*)

The original material reproduced on this and the preceding page was coloured.

# 4

## Some Practical Techniques for Pupils in the Field

IN the previous chapter we have discussed what may be called the teacher-led excursion, though we have tried to emphasize the vital role of pupil-investigation in such an excursion. There are a number of units of field-study, however, which pupils either individually or in groups can carry out on their own, and we now wish to offer some suggestions as to how such work may best be planned. Let it be clear that we are seeking to plan field-study which shall correspond in essence, though not in extent or depth, to the original field-work which a university student or even a research worker finds it necessary to do. At an advanced level, of course, field-work forms part of a larger whole, in which the use of records of different kinds will usually also be important. For the secondary-school pupil it is probably better to provide some opportunities for field-study which can be satisfying and reasonably complete in themselves without much additional material of a different kind. The value of such study as part of a true geographical training has already been stressed.

What constitutes good field-work? In brief, accurate observation accurately recorded. If this is to be achieved by boys and girls, perhaps of no more than average ability, we need to help them to plan and organize their work so that they know exactly what they seek to observe and exactly how they are going to record it. It is of little use sending them out with ill-defined objectives. Our experience of village studies, for example, suggests that a rather vague injunction to "find out what the village is like" leads to uncertain efforts in which direct observation gives place to the questioning of the local inhabitants. We recall some groups of teachers sent out to study various villages, with a good deal more indication than the sentence quoted above of what to look for, some of whom nevertheless came back with much dubious information obtained from the vicar or from the local publican. True, it had rained nearly all day. That was many years ago and we and they have learned better.

Suppose we have some groups of youngsters ready to study the village near which they are staying in camp or on a school journey : how shall we set them to work? First of all, let us accept the data already available—the map. There may be occasions for asking them to make a map, but amateur surveying does not constitute a village study. We suggest that the pupils should be provided with (duplicated) copies of a large-scale map of the village, at least 6-in., preferably 25-in. Here, we say in effect, is what is known already; now go and observe and record what is not already recorded. If we are seeking to establish the *character* of the village (as distinct for the moment from the *site*) we need a building-by-building record of it. We shall therefore probably arrive in discussion with the pupils at some such technique as this : number each building on the map and in a notebook or on a separate sheet record its character under a number of headings. These are the sorts of headings that have proved suitable in our experience :

A.  *The Building itself*

(1)  Age : say "old," "medium," or "new"; this is probably enough for younger pupils, but of course refinement is possible, and closer definition in discussion is desirable. However, we do not think more than three or four age categories helpful.

(2)   Material :

    (*a*)   roof
    (*b*)   upper storey(s)
    (*c*)   ground floor

This subdivision is necessary because so often the three parts are made of different materials.

B.   *The Use of the Building*

    (*a*)   upper storey(s)
    (*b*)   ground floor

The amount of possible detail here is considerable; we suggest that, for example, the *kind* of shop, if it is such, should be recorded.

If this information can be collected for all the buildings of the village, probably by groups or pairs of pupils doing a part of the village each, we shall have collectively the data for a reasonably satisfactory geographical appreciation of the village. The pupils can prepare, preferably on tracing-paper, a map of the distribution of buildings by age, and this is likely to show some sort of pattern. They can make maps of the shops and other non-residential buildings. They can arrive at some statistical analysis of the relative importance of different materials for roofing and for walls. What we may hope will have been their accurate observation accurately recorded in the field will yield a recognizable and presentable result likely to give them both satisfaction and an increased geographical understanding. Site studies are a little more advanced, and we prefer to leave that aspect of village field-work till near the end of this chapter.

What of farming? There is value in a straightforward land-use, or, still better, crop survey. If we are to ask a group of youngsters to record the crops of an area on the map we shall need to warn them very carefully not to do anything which may lead to trouble with the farmer. It is really necessary to have permission from farmers for this kind of work, and then to speak quite strongly to pupils about shutting gates and not walking on crops (including hay). If permission can be obtained a crop survey is often found interesting and again yields a useful and presentable result. Among the by-products of such work is a realization of what is really meant by inter-visibility and dead ground and of how in fact one cannot see far up a convex slope. A land-use survey too teaches, usually by bitter experience, that good map-reading and preliminary planning can save miles of walking.

Land-use is not the whole of farming, even if we add to crop survey the more uncertain recording of animals occupying pastures. There is in addition a legitimate kind of farm study which, perhaps unfortunately, involves asking questions of the farmer or of some one willing to speak for him—neither of them easy to find so often. As with the village study, it is essential for youngsters to set out with definite headings under which to record answers. The following is a list which may be lengthened or cut down according to circumstances :

A.  *The Farm Buildings*

    (1)  Site
    (2)  Building material
    (3)  How many buildings and of what kinds?

B.  *The Farm*

    (1)  Approximate size
    (2)  Kinds of land included
    (3)  General emphasis of the farming economy
    (4)  Cash crops
    (5)  Feed crops
    (6)  Common crop rotation
    (7)  Stock

| | | | |
|---|---|---|---|
| A | Up the scarp: unmetalled, unfenced lanes | | Lower dip slope: narrow, metalled lanes |
| B | Nil | Nil | Northern half only – evidence of afforestation. Beech plantations with occasional pines |
| C | Nil | Very old | Shooting house – brick. Keeper's cottage – flint, stone | Scattered farmhouses of flint and brick |
| D | Unused | Mixed cereals | Nil | 60% arable – cereals and roots. Small Friesian herds. |

Staplaash Farm

| | E | Lower chalk | Mid. chk | Upper | Chalk |
|---|---|---|---|---|---|
| F | | Hedgerow trees Ragwort | Mainly ash woodland with hawthorn | | Limited – mainly arable |
| G | | Smooth | Smooth | Circular hollows; chalk pits | |
| | | | | Rounded summits with dry valley bottoms, undulating country | |
| H | | Steep | concave | convex | |
| J | | White heavy loam | black, heavy Clay with flints? | Heavy soil of clay character | Light brown, light loamy character |
| K | | Nil | | Water-logged patches Swallets? | Some dew ponds. Water from rain collection and wells. Some piped from Staplaash Farm |

Arable    Pasture    Rough Pasture    Woodland

A — COMMUNICATIONS  B — NON-AGRICULTURAL OCCUPATIONS  C — SETTLEMENT  D — FARMING

E — GEOLOGY  F — VEGETATION  G — SURFACE CHARACTER  H — SLOPE  J — SOIL  K — HYDROLOGY & WATER SUPPLY

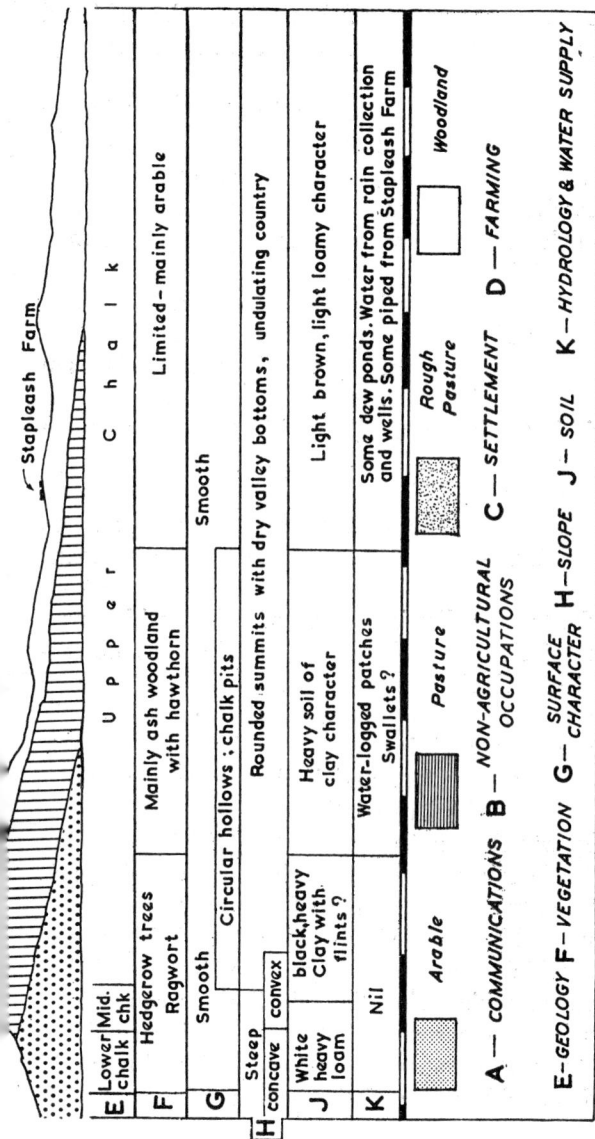

Fig. 4. A Transect across the South Downs in West Sussex

A very good co-operative piece of work can be achieved by co-ordinating farm studies of this kind with crop surveys done by other groups of pupils.

It may be felt suitable for older pupils to attempt in the field some geographical study of a many-sided character, in which, rather than concentrating on farming alone, an attempt is made to perceive and record interrelationships. A form of group work which has proved most rewarding has been termed the transect. In brief, this is a traverse along a belt of country during which land-use is recorded within the belt and observations of a variety of facts of physical and human geography noted in succession. The total of the observations is then "written up" in relation to a cross-section or profile along a central line within the belt, and observed facts from anywhere within the belt recorded against the appropriate point on the profile. It is generally convenient in preparing this final record to place the profile and the land-use belt centrally and to record items of human geography above these and items of physical geography below them (Figure 4). The key to the value of the transect lies in the use of a *belt*, which provides a variety of significant facts, instead of simply observing along a *line*, which would miss many of them. The transect naturally proves most profitable if attempted in terrain where there are clearly distinguishable varieties of geology, relief, and human occupation, and if the transect is run at right angles to the lie of such variations.

How exactly will the pupils work in the field in observing for a transect? We advocate groups of about four pupils, each group being given two or three miles of transect to cover in a day. The group will be supplied with a map, probably on the $2\frac{1}{2}$-in. scale, on which to record land-use. We have found that a belt 2 kilometres wide, using the grid lines, is convenient. The emphasis is upon ensuring that the central part of the section of the transect is completed in respect of land-use; odd marginal fields on either side of the belt may be ignored if

*Left:*
The leveller holds his ruler, with attached postcard to provide the right angle, towards the camera. The plumb-line can be seen. The left-hand boy indicates how far the ruler should be tilted so that it becomes horizontal.

*Below:*
The right-hand boy is the "levelling pole" and in this case has a marker on his back. He moves away until his marker comes into line with the horizontal sight-rule and he is then a known height above the leveller.

*Plate 2.* LEVELLING

These two photographs show the simple kind of levelling described in pages 50 and 51.

*Left:*

The leveller stands in the stream bed and is dealing with the long-profile of the stream, the "pole" being off to the left of the picture.

*Below:*

The cross-profile is being dealt with. The right-hand boy is the "pole" and the centre boy is the recorder, plotting on squared paper the results as they are called out. The sight-rule is being checked from the position of the photographer.

*Plate 3.* LEVELLING A STREAM PROFILE

they are found too difficult of access. The group will need to plan their work carefully nevertheless, and to divide their forces on either side of the central line from time to time. In addition to the map record notes are to be made of significant geographical details of all kinds. Each note is to be identified by a grid reference or at least a reference in terms of the grid to fix the position of the observation along the line of section. It is convenient to record facts of physical geography on the pages on one side of the notebook and facts of human geography on the opposite pages. Pupils will need more detailed headings, however, to stimulate them to accumulate sufficient data. We may suggest, for example, soil, drainage, slope, and nature of surface; vegetation, water supply, settlement sites, building material, type of farming, non-agricultural land-use, and evidence of non-agricultural occupations. As with the village survey, emphasis must be laid on direct observation rather than upon questioning "the locals." The subsequent writing-up of the data with the colouring of the land-use map and the drawing of the profile forms a satisfying sorting-out of material collected, and the final putting together of the contributions of the groups gives a result in which geographical pattern emerges if the transect has been well chosen.

There are certain other types of group work, more particularly on the physical aspects of geography, which have been found successful, and many of these involve the observation or measurement of slope. In passing we may remark that it is particularly salutary for boys and girls in the field to make exact observations of slope, since misconceptions about the true slopes of important geographical features, such as river profiles and scarps, one might say are inculcated in their minds by the vertically exaggerated diagrams of textbooks at any level from that of the primary school to the university.

While there is in certain types of country useful work to be done in the plotting of significant breaks of slope such as that at the edge of the river terrace on a $2\frac{1}{2}$-in. or 6-in. map, the

basic piece of group work in all such studies may be regarded
as the direct levelling of the slope itself. This may sound
advanced, but we have found in practice that it is very possible
for pupils to make and record directly in the field a fairly exact
measurement of slope.

It may be best first of all to suggest the method and then
to go on to give examples of its application. A levelling team
should consist of three or four pupils, one of whom constitutes
the levelling staff. He may be marked off in feet as necessary.
A second member of the team employs a primitive clinometer,
made by attaching a protractor or a postcard to a ruler, which
forms the sighting level, and attached to which a plumb-bob
enables the ruler to be held horizontal by use of the protractor
or postcard. A third member of the team, standing at right
angles to the second, will have the job of seeing that the ruler
is held at right angles to the plumb-line. This member or the
fourth member of the team will act as the recorder. Starting
from a datum point (see Plate 2, p. 48), the leveller (No. 2) in-
structs the levelling pole (No. 1) to move away from him
up the slope to such a distance that an agreed interval of
height separates them. The distance between them is then
paced out and the result recorded direct on squared paper by
counting along the horizontal distance in paces (yards) and the
vertical distance up *at the same scale*. A practicable scale is
one-tenth of an inch to a yard, on which scale it is possible to
use a vertical difference of height between members 1 and 2
of the team of one foot or three feet, and to plot the distance
between them in paces or yards as a square per yard.

We have found it particularly profitable to profile the slope
of a stream bed by this method; it may be done either along
the bank or at the foot of the bank at river level. Generally
speaking, the leveller and the pole may as well decide to get
their feet wet from the start (Plate 3, p. 49).

If a stream course is divided out among several groups
working in this way, and the sections covered by each carefully

Fig. 5. RIVER STUDY

This is a reproduction of pupils' work. On the profile vertical and horizontal scales of both long profile and cross-sections are the same (one small square: 5 yd.). (See p. 52.)

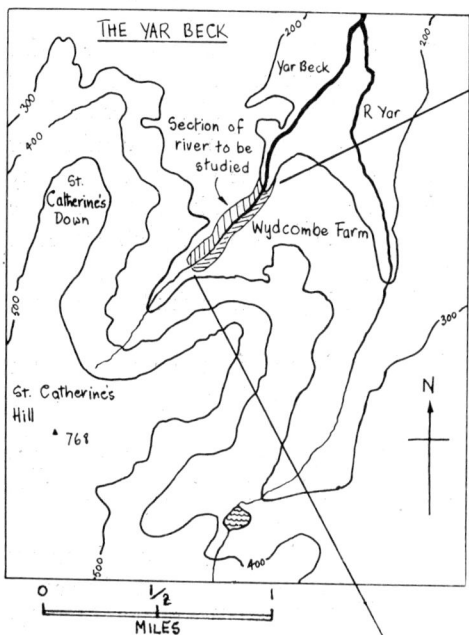

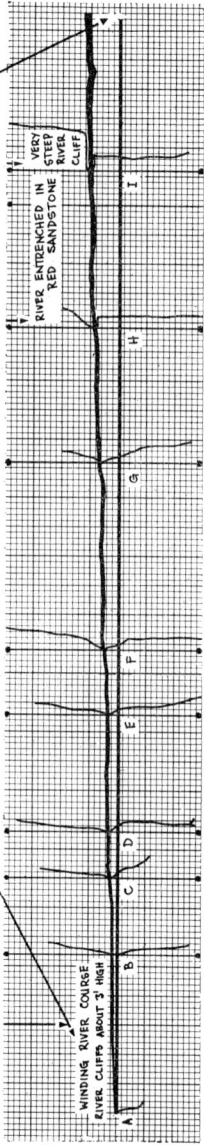

RIVER PROFILE

associated to one another by the use of contours on the $2\frac{1}{2}$-in. map, a day's work by half a dozen groups can produce a fair length of profile which will give significant differences of slope in relation to the nature of the valley and of the terrain over which the stream passes. The very gentle slopes revealed by most such exercises in this country will be a helpful corrective to the impression given by the diagrams on this subject, even in our academic papers.

It is also profitable and interesting to make similar measurements of the slopes of the sides of the valley (Plate 3), and these may be done at the same time and on the same graph paper by turning the paper through a right angle and using the verticals of the long-profile as the horizontal bases of these cross-profiles. The total result of the groups working in this way will therefore be to give a series of varied cross-sections correctly sited in relation to the long profile of the stream (Figure 5). Simple levelling of this kind can be used in many situations to give, for example, a true measurement of a scarp, of a river-terrace edge, or indeed of any feature local to the school which will help to bring exactness as well as a sense of reality into the pupils' appreciation of the significance of slope. Clearly such measurements of slope, when associated with a continuous feature such as a river terrace, may well be linked up with the plotting of the break of slope in plan.

We have found it particularly helpful to make use of this simple levelling method together with landscape sketching and the plotting of additional data on a large-scale map to bring exactness into the study of the site of an old settlement. The legendary pupil who told the inspector that if he knew where the town was he would explain why it was there, would, we fear, have had to rely upon one of a few general explanations of the siting of settlements which he would have heard of in his geography lessons and which do not always stand up to examination in the field. The famous spring-line settlements at the foot of the chalk scarps, for example, are often not exactly on a spring or even on a stream at all. The careful examination of a farm or village will often reveal its relationship to some significant though small breaks of slope or flattening of the terrain which cannot be observed from the printed map, and indeed are often overlooked in the field unless an exact measurement of slope is made.

This study of site seems to us to be of a truly geographical character, and the kind of group work we are now thinking of to be the expression in practical field-work of the dictum that geography consists of the evaluation of the place factor in human affairs. We readily give our pupils training in the interpretation of large-scale topographical maps, asking them to discover from such maps the significant features of the siting of human settlement. Nevertheless, in many cases the maps necessarily fail to give the significant factor which can only be observed in the field and which calls for the exact measurement of slope to record it. The technique by which a group of about four pupils may be asked to analyse the site, say, of an old farm, will therefore consist of three elements. First, a general reconnaissance of the site, at which stage the members of the team would make a few landscape sketches of the site as seen from two or three different vantage points; secondly, this reconnaissance would suggest perhaps three or four lines along which an exact levelling might be carried out, some of which might reveal significant changes of slope; and the third element would consist of a large-scale sketch-plan of the site area on which would be marked the points from which the landscape sketches had been made, the lines along which the sections had been drawn, and the position of any important breaks of slope revealed by them. A team of four who have had some practice in levelling will be able to make a satisfactory and detailed study of a site within a day, or, in some cases, a good deal less. This technique of site study is best practised to begin with in relation to a single settlement, in fairly open country, but its application to village study by

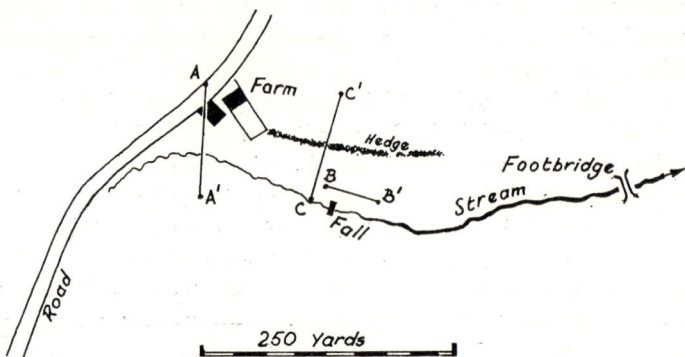

Fig. 6 (*a*). GENERAL PLAN OF THE FARM SITE, SHOWING POSITION OF
SURVEYED PROFILES

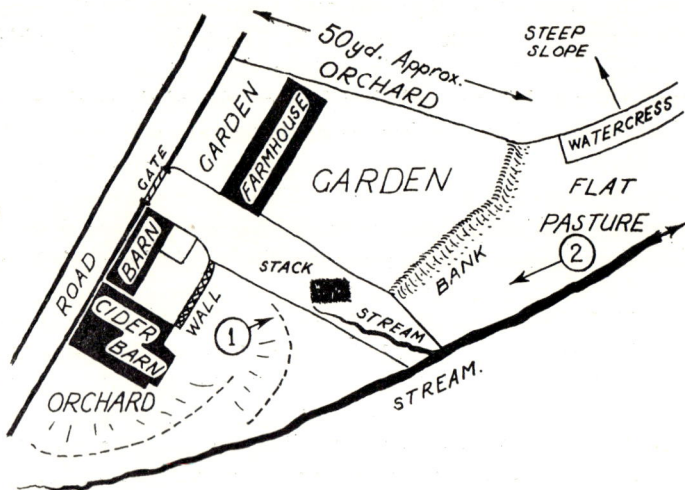

Fig. 6 (*b*). SKETCH PLAN OF FARM SITE DRAWN ON THE SPOT, SHOWING
SIGNIFICANT SLOPES AND THE POSITION FROM WHICH SKETCHES WERE
MADE

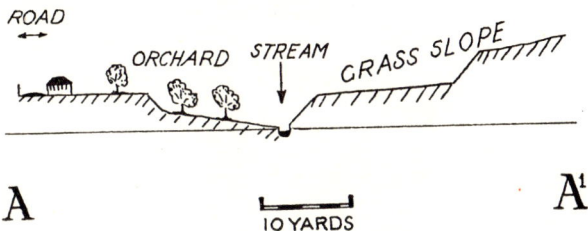

Fig. 6 (c). SKETCH SECTION AT FARM SITE, TRUE VERTICAL SCALE, LEVELLED AND PLOTTED ON THE SPOT. COMPARE Fig. 6 (a), SHOWING POSITION OF SECTION, AND Fig. 6 (b), SHOWING BREAKS OF SLOPE IN PLAN

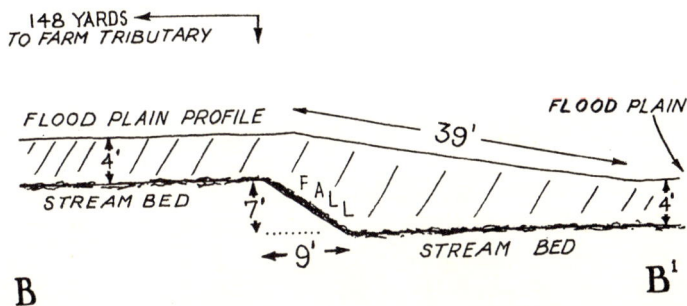

Fig. 6 (d). SKETCH SECTIONS (TRUE VERTICAL SCALE) SHOWING RELATIONSHIP BETWEEN STREAM BED PROFILE AND FLOOD PLAIN PROFILE AT THE BREAK OF THE SLOPE RELATING TO THE UPPER GREENSAND EDGE. COMPARE Fig. 6 (a) FOR POSITION OF SECTION

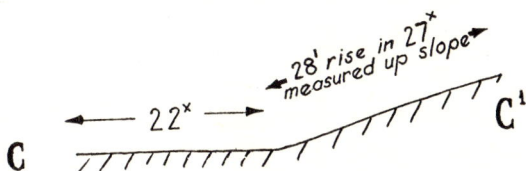

Fig. 6 (e). FLOOD PLAIN AND VALLEY SIDE SECTION NEAR FALL (COMPARE Fig. 6 (a))

Fig. 6 (f). FIELD SKETCH MADE FROM (1) ON Fig. 6 (b)

Labels in figure:

Stream

break of slope relating to fall

flat pasture

Slope C

slope to stream

water access

Stack

Tributary Stream

Orchard

Orchard

Garden

Farm House

gdn

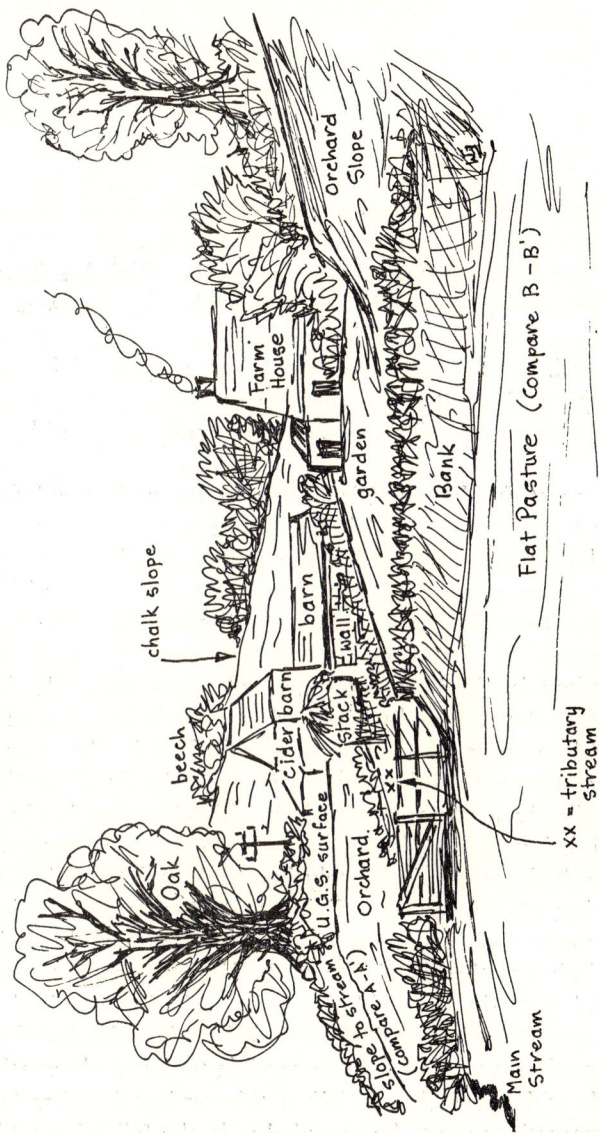

chalk slope

beech

Oak

Cider barn

barn

wall

stack

Farm House

garden

orchard

U.G.S. surface

slope to stream (compare A–A')

Main Stream

Orchard Slope

Bank

Flat Pasture (Compare B–B')

xx = tributary stream

Fig. 6 (g). FIELD SKETCH MADE FROM (2) ON Fig. 6 (b)

a team with some experience will be obvious. (Figure 6—The sketches set out to give an analysis, made in the field, of the exact site of a farm which in general terms lies on the Upper Greensand bench at the foot of the chalk scarp of the Western South Downs, and bears some relationship to the "spring line." The plans, profiles, and landscape sketches are closely interrelated, and should be compared carefully the one with the other.)

A quite different type of physical study which has interest and value is that of soil. The soil is the link between the vegetation cover, the varieties in which we would expect to be observed by our pupils in the field, and the underlying rock which forms the material of the hills and valleys, whose shapes we often tell our pupils are being continually modified by the forces of denudation, transportation, and deposition. One of the most fundamental concepts to be understood from practical work in the field is this of the temporary character of the landscape as we see it : a condition of balance in terms of vegetation, a stage different from an earlier one and itself changing towards another stage developing from the plant associations of the present time; a state of temporary equilibrium in the mass movement of waste material which constitutes the process by which slopes are being continually modified; a stage of temporary equilibrium in the streams, whose courses are continually changing, gradually all the time, spasmodically in times of flood. In this changing landscape the soil, being the transition zone between the vegetation cover and the bed rock, is intimately involved, and to understand something of the soil as a living and changing cover is to make more real what tends to be our rather theoretical appreciation of the mutability of the land forms. In terms of practical work in the field this means digging a soil-pit in which a cross-section of the layers of the soil and sub-soil can be exposed as a vertical face susceptible to direct observation. A spade width is sufficient. When this vertical face has been cut, observations are to be recorded as in the following table :

OBSERVATIONS RELATING TO THE WHOLE SOIL-PIT

| Profile No.: I, II, III . . . | Locality: | Site: | Vegetation: |
|---|---|---|---|
| Map Reference: Six-figure co-ordinates | General description | e.g., Summit, slope, lowland | Including state of cultivation |

OBSERVATIONS RELATING TO EACH HORIZON SEPARATELY

| Horizon | Depth in cm. | Clarity | Colour | Organic matter | Roots | Texture | Mineral skeleton | | Water conditions | pH | CO3 |
|---|---|---|---|---|---|---|---|---|---|---|---|
| | | | | | | | Size | Amount | | | |
| 1 | | Between horizons: sharp, clear, i.e., merging < 3 cm., clear 3 to 5 cm., merging over 5 cm. | | In tenths or plentiful, some, little, nil | Plentiful, some, little, nil | See table below | Large, medium, small | Plentiful, some, little, nil | Saturated, wet, damp, dry, very dry | | |
| 2 | | | | | | | | | | | |
| etc. | | | | | | | | | | | |

KEY FOR SOIL TEXTURE IDENTIFICATION[1]

| 1 | Soil feels gritty ... ... ... 2 |
| | Soil not gritty ... ... ... 4 |
| 2 | Soil will form a cohesive ball ... Light Loam |
| | Soil will not form a cohesive ball ... 3 |
| 3 | Soil stains the fingers ... ... Heavy Sand |
| | Soil does not stain the fingers ... Light Sand |
| 4 | Soil silky or sticky ... ... 5 |
| | Soil neither silky nor sticky ... Loam |
| 5 | Soil will not polish when rubbed between the fingers ... ... ... ... 6 |
| | Soil will polish when rubbed between the fingers ... ... ... ... 7 |
| 6 | Soil just slightly silky ... ... Silty Loam |
| | Soil markedly silky ... ... Light Silt |
| 7 | Soil very difficult to deform between finger and thumb ... ... ... Clay |
| | Soil not very difficult to deform ... 8 |
| 8 | Soil resistant but fairly easily deformed ... Medium Loam |
| | Soil deformed with some difficulty ... Heavy Loam |

Based on The Study of Soil, by J. M. Branson, B.Sc. (School Nature Study Union, Publication No. 22, 1950).

[1]The soil *must* be moistened to give conditions suitable for the test.

Some of the observations must be made in the field, others must be done indoors; some, such as texture and colour, may be made either at the time or later. It is often interesting and helpful to produce to scale a soil colour strip by smearing some of the moist soil from each layer on to a strip of stout paper marked off in lengths corresponding, say, at half-scale to the actual depths of the horizons. Some further interesting suggestions for soil study are made in the pamphlet published by the School Nature Study Union.[1]

In the field, of course, the subjects usually taught separately in the school run together, and in the study of the soil is an excellent opportunity for co-operation between the geography and science departments. In particular, the ascertainment of the pH value[2] of samples of soil from each of the horizons exposed calls for help from the chemistry lab. It is not a difficult matter for the chemists to produce, say, six or eight buffer solutions varying in colour from blue through green, yellow, and orange to red, corresponding to known pH values in relation to a standard universal soil indicator. A small sample of soil is mixed with a few drops of indicator, the coloured liquid thus produced carefully drained off, and diluted with distilled water, to a transparency comparable with that of the buffer solutions, and its colour compared with that of the buffer solutions. It is not difficult to arrive at pH values with an accuracy of ·1, and an interesting and often significant difference of pH value between the different horizons in one soil-pit can be observed, and between different soil-pits if these are in contrasted positions or on different rocks or on areas of different land-use. In rugged country significant relationships between vegetation, soil, and slope will often be shown by a combination of levelling, soil study and a vegetation transect. Needless to say, it is desirable to seek permission

[1] Reference as in table on page 59.
[2] The pH value is a measure of the acid (or alkaline) reaction of the soil.

before digging a soil-pit on cultivated land. A rough test for carbonate may be made with dilute HCl., sufficient to give a descriptive result, "much," "some," "nil."

It may be observed that most of the practical techniques of study in the field we have described depend upon pupils working together in small teams and, in a number of cases, upon those teams working together to produce a corporate result. Beside the geographical value of such methods we hold it not unimportant that the training in geographical investigation is also a training in co-operation, and illustrates the way in which an interesting and significant result can often only be achieved by groups of people working together on an agreed plan.

# 5

## Field-work in Towns

WE have spoken so far chiefly of the countryside. Most teachers would probably agree that whatever the nature of the locality which includes the pupil's home and school, it should provide material to help in the effective teaching of the subject. The local region can be used for comparison; it is the standard of reference, the measuring-rod, whose use can ensure the better understanding by pupils of environments different from their own. The good teacher can demonstrate that geography concerns real things in a real environment by frequent reference to familiar features and to the experiences of the pupils.

Perhaps it is not generally realized that for more than 80 per cent. of the school-children of Britain the home region is essentially an urban one: a region which often consists of closely packed houses, factories, and shops, including busy streets and markets, and with population densities which may attain 17,000 to the square mile in Manchester or 30,000 per square mile in parts of central London. Such areas abound with material useful for purposes of comparison. The breadth of the local river, the size of the canal lock, the average annual rainfall (and the number of rain-days), the population of the town or borough, are a few examples of a numerical nature, but comparison may also be made between local manufacturing processes and the village craft work of India or China, or between means of transport, building materials, and food-stuffs at home with those of distant lands.

Undoubtedly the nature of the urban environment restricts the range of possible comparison, and for this reason, if for no other, the vitalizing and stimulating influences of the periodic rural excursion are essential. But it would be wrong to assume that field-work is possible only in a rural area; much sound geographical study can be profitably undertaken in the immediate surroundings of any school, and on a more restricted scale urban field-work can demonstrate the techniques, and do something to engender the "geographical" attitude towards features of the earth's surface which are necessary in any field-study.

As in the rural area, the urban teacher can encourage in pupils habits of thoughtful observation which, linked with large-scale map study and careful methods of recording, will co-ordinate and consolidate the haphazard knowledge which most town children have about their localities. Children are very ready to watch workmen digging a deep hole in the road near school but suggestion from the observant teacher will probably be necessary before they notice the nature of the excavated material. Similarly pupils may observe lorries laden with iron-bound, hessian-wrapped bales travelling along a main road away from the docks without appreciating the significance of the fact that the lorries belong to a Bradford firm. Training in thoughtful observation should be one important aim in urban study. Encouragement in observation and frequent reference to the locality for comparative purposes should be features of the geography courses of both primary and secondary schools. But at some stage in a course it may be possible to attempt more continuous, systematic investigation of the urban environment. For example, during their last year in the school those pupils not taking an external examination often become blasé and bored; they are looking outward, away from the school, to the life which appears to have the attraction of freedom and independence. The interest of these pupils can be captured more successfully if all the work attempted in school can be made to bear some relationship to the lives they expect to be leading in the near future. This orientation is possible with most of the usual school subjects, and it is particularly true of geography which, treated in its widest sense, should aim to show the part any individual can play as a useful member of a community. A systematic study of the locality during the last year can contribute towards this desirable end and capture the interests of the pupils. In small groups during school time, supervised perhaps at first, then on their own, pupils can set about the planned collection of information on the immediate locality of the school.

At this stage the study of the urban area can provide the means for demonstrating geographical principles to an extent not generally realized. The essence of geography is the study of the relationships between distributions, and this is as possible, although less apparent, in the urban area as in the rural. What sort of material should be collected and recorded and studied? The traffic census may be considered as an example. The pupils record the numbers of vehicles of different types and their direction of movement at certain places and at different times of the day. Such activity requires the making of an accurate record, and the portrayal of the information in a suitable chart, and, no doubt, there is some value in the completion of these two stages. But the real geographical significance of the work comes from the discussion of the conclusions which may be drawn from the evidence; the types of traffic which preponderate, the nature of the loads as far as they may be determined, the direction of the loaded vehicles, comparison between traffic on different roads or on the same road at different times, and so on. The attempt to find explanations can be a valuable mental stimulus. The mapping of the positions of letter-boxes and telephone-kiosks in a given area provides an easy distributional exercise, but this can be

*Plate 4.* AN AUSTRALIAN DROVER

*By courtesy of Australian News Information Bureau*

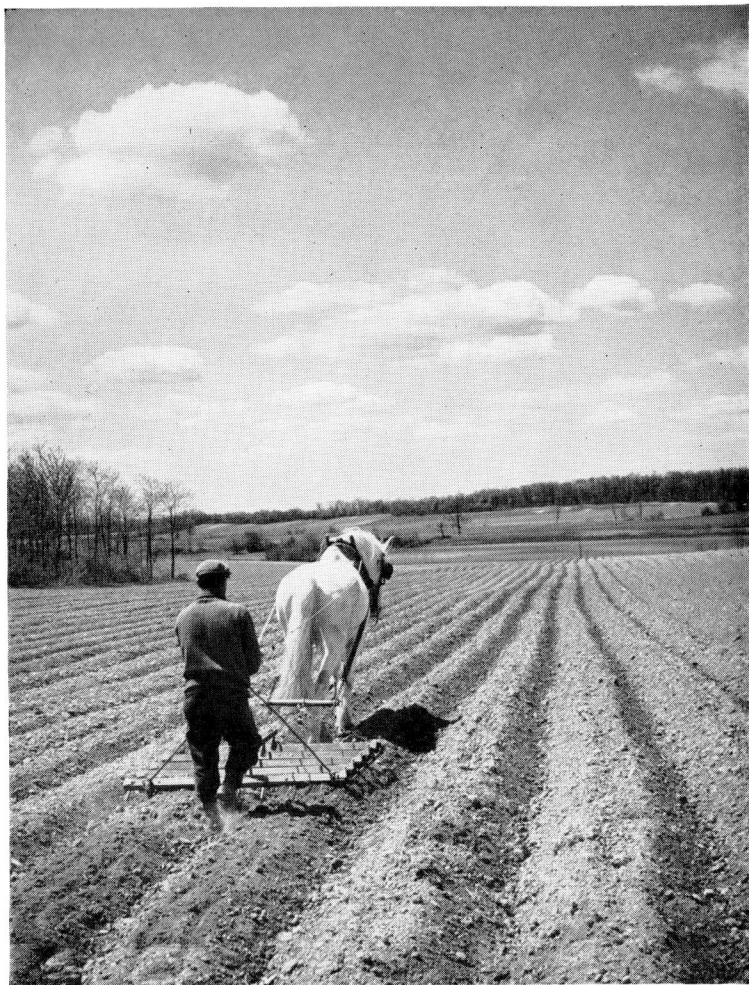

*Plate 5.* FARMING ON LONG ISLAND, U.S.A.

*Photograph by Ewing Galloway*

[*See page* 121.]

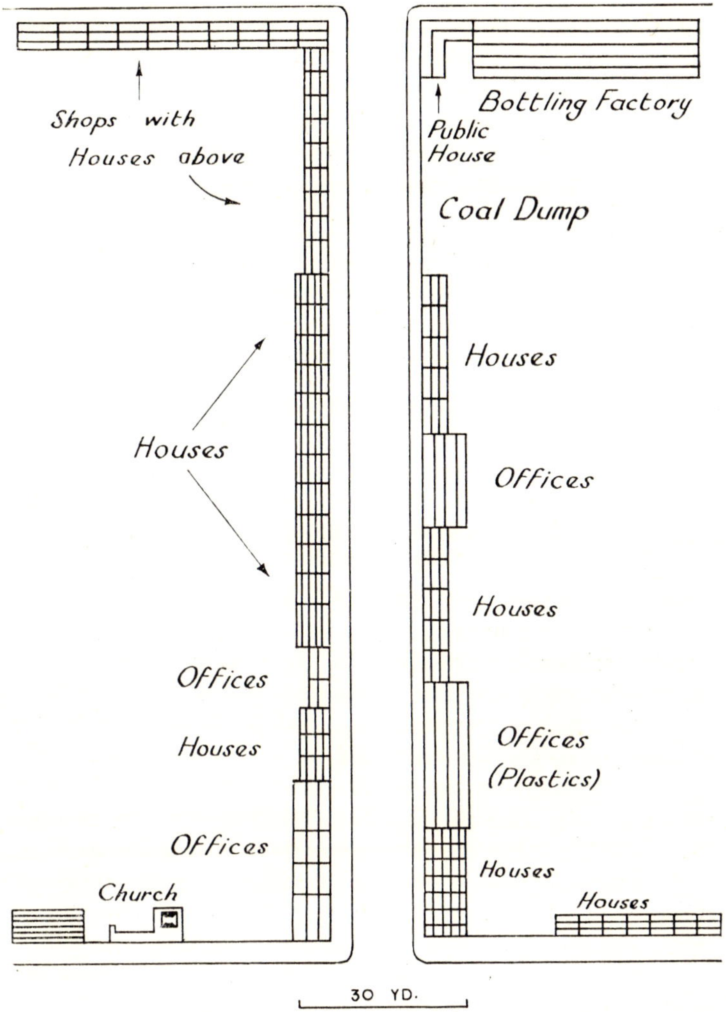
Shops with
Houses above
Houses
Offices
Houses
Offices
Church
Bottling Factory
Public
House
Coal Dump
Houses
Offices
Houses
Offices
(Plastics)
Houses
Houses
30 YD.

Fig. 7. Streets in Central London

of limited value unless followed by discussion and comment on the result. Letter-boxes may occur with greater frequency at street junctions and in busy commercial areas than elsewhere; telephone-kiosks may be more widely spaced in the very wealthy residential areas and in the very poor.

Such work therefore falls into four clearly defined stages:

(1) The planning and organization of the investigation
(2) Observation and recording
(3) Display or demonstration of the results
(4) Consideration of the evidence with discussion and an attempt to reach some conclusions

Some aspects of urban geographical study are valuable and rewarding but less obvious. For example, the close study of a few streets in the immediate neighbourhood of the school in order to gather accurate detail on shops, factories, houses and other buildings can provide useful material for mapping and discussion. The pupils are provided with a duplicated map, on as large a scale as possible, which shows only the streets. Figure 7 shows a method which has been employed by some London schools for recording the location of buildings and the number of floors. The frontage is shown by the distance along the street, in the usual way, and the floors are indicated by lines parallel to the street, one for each floor from the first upward. A basement can be shown by a dotted line between the street edge and the first line. Buildings can be grouped into a small number of categories as illustrated in Figure 8 (a), and the effectiveness of the map is enhanced if the types are distinguished by colour. In the map showing the number of floors coloured lines could be employed to indicate the utilization of the floors; three black lines above a red frontage line might indicate, for example, a shop with a three-floored dwelling above. Another possibility derives from this method. The National Census Return gives the average number of occupants per room, in each town or borough. The recording

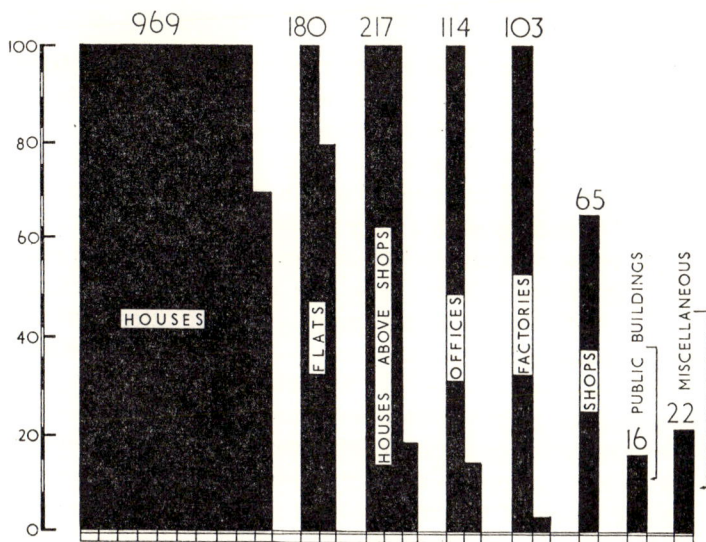

Fig. 8 (a). CENSUS OF BUILDINGS IN PART OF A LONDON BOROUGH. THE
103 FACTORIES ARE BROKEN DOWN INTO CATEGORIES IN Fig 8 (b)

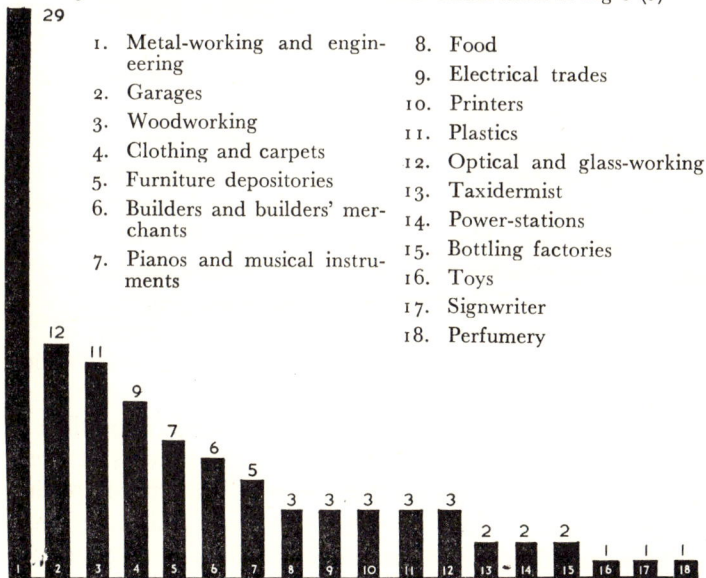

1. Metal-working and engineering
2. Garages
3. Woodworking
4. Clothing and carpets
5. Furniture depositories
6. Builders and builders' merchants
7. Pianos and musical instruments
8. Food
9. Electrical trades
10. Printers
11. Plastics
12. Optical and glass-working
13. Taxidermist
14. Power-stations
15. Bottling factories
16. Toys
17. Signwriter
18. Perfumery

Fig. 8 (b). CENSUS OF FACTORIES IN PART OF A LONDON BOROUGH

of the floors makes it easy to assess the approximate number of rooms in the house and consequently the number of people living in a street or a block of buildings. The material is thus available for the construction of a population distribution map for any small urban area. Pupils would see the problems attached to making such a map and would be in a position to assess more accurately the deficiencies of the population maps shown in school atlases. From the constructed map many valuable deductions and explanations may be attempted and possible relationships worked out—for example, the position of small shopping centres near to pockets of dense population, distances from means of transport and forms of entertainment, the concentration of the male inhabitants in one neighbouring place of work or their scattering to many places.

In the course of this investigation the position of factories, warehouses, garages, shops, cinemas, public-houses, etc., will have been mapped. Note will have been made of the nature of the occupation in the factories and the kind of raw materials employed. Charts can then be constructed to show the number of buildings in given categories and the nature of the work in the factories, as in Figure 8 (*b*), which shows the results of a similar investigation carried out over nearly ninety acres of a densely populated London borough. The preponderance of certain industries—*e.g.*, metal-working and wood-working (with furniture-making), is most striking. Discussion could centre round possible explanations for this specialization and the sources of raw material and its transport, while a useful follow-up could include visits to the more important or the more educationally useful firms, or discussion of information supplied by the firms themselves.

A rather different type of distributional study is possible in the newer suburban areas which lie on the borders of great cities. An example on the northern edge of London, comprising a small shopping centre serving a good-class residential area, has been investigated and the map of the district is reproduced in Figure 9. A census of the shops gives the result shown in Figure 10, which demonstrates the preponderance of those selling foodstuffs and the less essential services such as hairdressing, florists, and newsagents-tobacconists, which such an area would require near at hand. Examination and discussion of these results would bring out that these are all small shops catering for the day-to-day needs of the immediate locality; larger, more expensive items are bought in the big shopping centres of the neighbourhood where there will be greater variety of choice, more competition, and somewhat lower prices.

The validity of such deductions can be demonstrated by consideration of the locality with regard to transport facilities and to distances. The small shopping centre illustrated lies on the edge of a plateau whose steeply descending western side is almost covered with houses. People on the lower half of this slope will go mainly to a large shopping centre in the valley, which is served by a bus route. Those on the eastern side of the main road, and some distance from it, will tend to use the large easterly shopping centre, which is well served by a bus route. These and other deductions can be drawn from the investigation and recording of distributional data of this nature; geographical relationships can be demonstrated even in the most unlikely areas.

In suburban districts thought-provoking distribution maps may be compiled to show the period of building as in the village survey of the last chapter. In a district which has developed since the Industrial Revolution the periods might be: pre-1800, nineteenth century, 1900–39, post-1945. The style of architecture (an interesting study in itself) will be a guide to the age: some houses are dated, and in cases of doubt an estate agent will usually be prepared to help with information. Examination of the map will show how the settlement was first located and the direction of its growth relative to such factors as relief, main roads, and the advent of the railway.

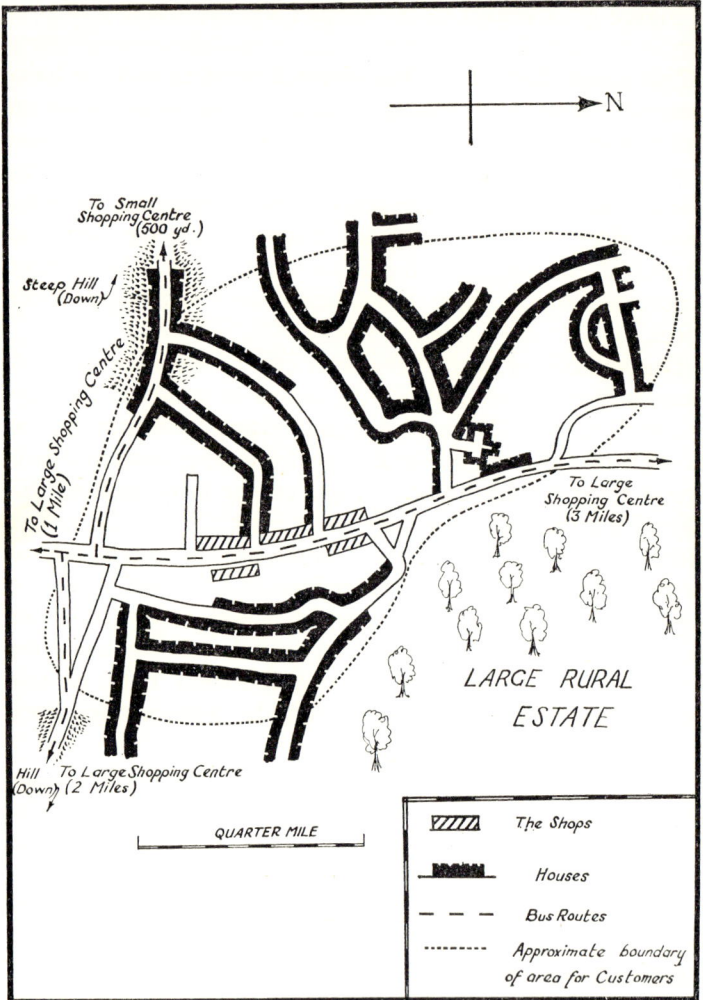

Fig. 9. A SUBURBAN SHOPPING CENTRE

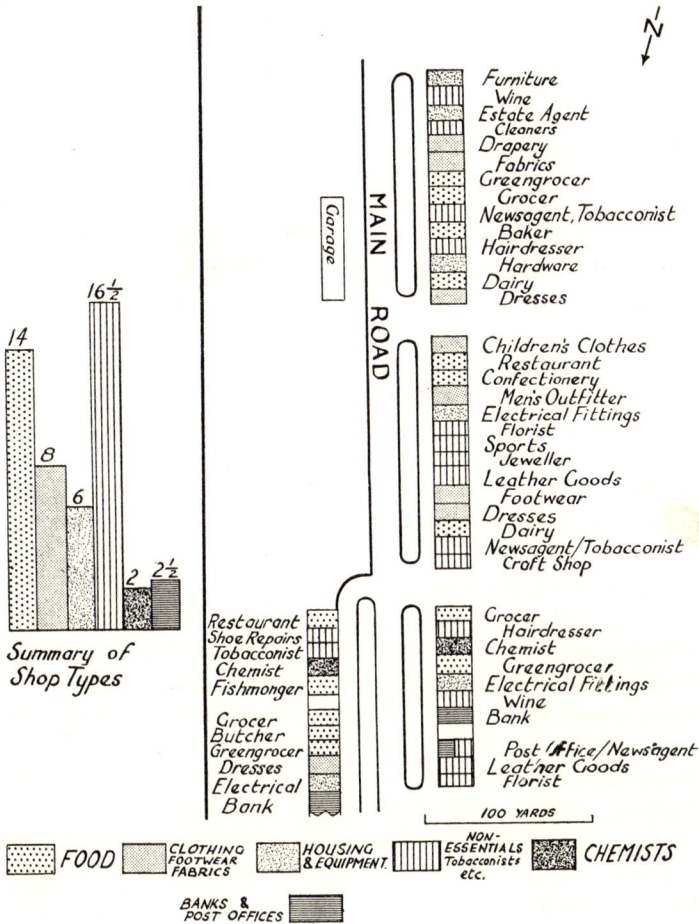

Fig. 10. Shops in a Suburban Shopping Centre

Although more difficult, the study of topographical features in a large urban area is not impossible. All the features of urban development—houses, shops, factories, roads, and railways—had to be placed on the earth's surface more or less as nature left it. Man makes some modifications in the surface features but only where this is absolutely essential, and the amount of "made ground" in an urban area is comparatively small, and confined to a few localities. Closely packed buildings tend to obscure relief features, and pupils miss changes in level especially when they are very slight. Railway cuttings, embankments and tunnels, canal locks emphasize major differences; minor gradients can be related to the presence of a few steps from a street level to a passageway, the position of the ground floors of certain houses relative to the road, the direction water flows in the gutter or the tendency of certain drains to flood after heavy rain. Sometimes it is helpful to demonstrate the gradient of a street by reference to the spot heights on the 25-in. or 6-in. Ordnance Survey plans or by application of the system of levelling described in the last chapter, and this may be linked with the fascinating task of reconstructing the distribution of the original drainage pattern. Confirmation of the positions of former water courses sometimes comes from street names, and certainly from the surveyor of the Local Government office whose maps will show many streams relegated to sewers. The recognition of relief features, such as small plateaux, ridges or valleys, beneath the cloak of dense urban development is a fascinating activity, and is important because it can help in the appreciation of the factors which were operative in the siting of the original settlement.

The question has been raised as to what area is best included in a systematic study of an urban locality. If statistics are to be used, then an administrative unit—an urban district or a borough—is desirable, but generally a large area—for example, a London borough—is too complex and congested for satisfactory study. An interesting and realistic method of defining the area to be considered is to plot on a large-scale map the homes of the pupils in the class. A line enclosing all the points marked, adjusted, perhaps, to run along the nearest streets, could then define the area, and would be very properly the "home region."

A new housing estate at first sight would appear to be an unrewarding area for study. No doubt the range of activities is reduced but many of the aspects mentioned above can be included. Studies of the distribution and types of houses, the building materials, means of communication, the transport of commodities, the facilities, the nature and distribution of shops, are all possible, and very often the buildings are sufficiently dispersed to permit easy study of relief, drainage pattern, and soils. First-hand geographical investigation of some kind is possible in any urban area.

# 6

## Outdoor Work on the School Premises

IN the preceding chapters we have stressed the importance of field-work in country and town but we would also emphasize that there is much good practical geography to be done in the school playground or playing-field. Reference is made elsewhere to survey[1] and to map study but among other important activities are observations of the sun and of the weather.

Although the foundations are often well laid in the primary school, most secondary pupils need to have their ideas on earth movement in relation to time and the seasons clarified and extended. The apparent movement of the sun can best be considered by the measurement of the length of shadow cast by an object such as a net-ball post or flagstaff. The shadow should be measured in the view of the class at about the same hour once a month for a year and the results recorded in the notebook for use in demonstrating the relationship between the altitude of the sun and the seasons. The fundamental concept needs to be stressed with all pupils, for misconceptions are easy, and some who have studied the subject beyond "O" level have been known to suggest that the summer occurs when the earth is nearest the sun! As a corollary, discussion can bring out the variation in the positions of the rising and setting sun through the year so that the pupil, with Rousseau's Emile, may exclaim, "So there is a summer east and a winter

[1] In Chapter 4, p. 50 and Chapter 9, p. 106.

east."[1] Similar measurements during the day may serve to introduce the movement of the earth on its axis and the subject of time.

The shadow of the post at noon (Greenwich Time) is useful for fixing the position of the north–south line when discussing the cardinal points and map orientation. Scale in maps, too, can be conveniently introduced by reference to the playground, for it is a very practical problem which demands a plan of such an area on a given sheet of paper.

A very worthwhile activity out of doors within the school precincts is the study of one of the most important of geographical elements—the weather. No pupil should pass through any secondary school without having had the experience of participating in some form of weather observation, for the reasons adduced in previous chapters for investigating the surface of the earth at first hand apply equally strongly to its atmosphere. In weather study may be demonstrated again the scientific approach which involves accurate observation, careful recording, consideration of the results, and deductions from them. British weather is so variable that it never lacks interest; moreover, our pupils are now made very weather-conscious, and become familiar with some of the technical terms through their acquaintance with weather maps on the television screen and in some daily newspapers.

This aspect of school geography may be carried out at a number of levels. At the top is the well-equipped weather station organized to provide continuous and frequent records, which may perhaps supply information for the official service. This is valuable and interesting work, making heavy demands on the enthusiasm and devotion of the participants. The method of setting up such a station, the apparatus required, and the routine of observation, are laid down in the publications of the Meteorological Office. For a variety of reasons

[1] Quoted in *Rousseau on Education*, R. L. Archer (Arnold, 1928), p. 151.

many geography teachers are unable to maintain a weather station to provide continuous records but valuable work can still be done over shorter periods and with a smaller range of equipment.

A Stevenson Screen is desirable though not essential, but it can be made in the school quite easily.[1] Basic instruments are the rain-gauge with its measuring cylinder, a maximum and minimum (Sixes) thermometer, a wind vane, and a barometer. A sunshine recorder, if it can be easily procured and maintained, is useful. The wet and dry bulb thermometer has been omitted because the humidity cannot be read off directly, and its function may be too difficult for some pupils, but those who can understand it should use it.

Whenever possible the work should be begun in the first year and could provide opportunity to handle the apparatus and learn how it works. Quite young pupils can appreciate the idea of measuring rainfall in inches especially if the principle is demonstrated graphically. The mathematics of the relationship between the diameters of funnel and measuring cylinder is unnecessary at first, although the reasons for using two pieces of apparatus and not one is a useful mental exercise. The working of the Sixes thermometer is simple to explain provided the function of the mercury as an indicator only is stressed. Normal temperatures will of course be taken in the shade but it is important that pupils should register for themselves the contrast between sun and shade temperatures and for this an ordinary thermometer is adequate.

Wind direction is easily observed but some may feel that measurement of wind speed is desirable also. Home-made forms of anemometer have been constructed but the easiest method of securing a guide to wind speed in the absence of instrumental means is to use the Beaufort Scale, modified to give the effects of wind force on objects on land—for example,

[1] *Stevenson Thermometer Screen: Instructions for Making* (H.M.S.O.).

when the wind speed near the earth's surface is from one to three miles an hour its direction is indicated by smoke drift but not by the wind vane; a speed of nineteen to twenty-four miles per hour, called a "fresh" wind, makes small trees in leaf begin to sway. This and much other valuable information on weather observation may be obtained from the *Meteorological Glossary* (H.M.S.O.).

Variation in atmospheric pressure is an important element in weather study, and it is essential that pupils should start with sound ideas about the nature and consequences of air pressure. A few simple experiments to demonstrate that air exerts pressure because it has weight may be desirable to begin with. Many pupils appear to have a clearer idea about the subject if they see the construction of the simple barometer; the closed tube completely filled with mercury excluding all air, the inversion of the tube with the finger over the open end, the open end placed beneath the surface of a bowl of mercury, the finger removed, the fall of the mercury and its vibration up and down as it presses against the equalizing force exerted by the air—the demonstration can teach far more than many words. In the absence of better apparatus the simple barometer may be used for the weather study, but the most effective instrument is, of course, the barograph, for then the variations are visibly demonstrated. For junior pupils readings in inches are easiest to comprehend, especially if the approach has been through the use of the simple mercury barometer.

Cloud observation is a much neglected aspect of weather study in schools. The main types of cloud should be described, observed, and nomenclature agreed upon. Senior pupils should use the technical terms but juniors might provide their own descriptive names; one class quickly proffered on various occasions, "pillow clouds," "wispy cloud," "rain cloud," and so on. Directed observation will soon show that the cloud cover frequently consists of a variety of types and that the outlines of some clouds—*e.g.*, cumulus, change considerably if watched for a few minutes. This can lead eventually to further discussion on the nature of cloud, the importance of vertical upward currents, and the occurrence of thunderstorms. Some might wish to record the proportion of sky covered with cloud but this is more difficult and less important; an agreed collection of phrases such as "a little cloud," "very cloudy," etc., might suffice.

After the apparatus has been demonstrated and the elements to be observed discussed, the next step is to organize the observers and agree on the form of record. Individual records are possible but the large chart, in an accessible place and filled in by each observer in turn, is easier to manage. On a large sheet of squared paper the elements are recorded to scale, one below the other, with differing forms of graph for each. Lines of different colour may be used for temperatures and pressures, bars or columns for rainfall, a line appropriately oriented to show wind direction, with arrows attached to indicate speed, a simple diagrammatic indication of the nature of cloud, and so on. The readings may be taken once a day at about the same time for as long a period as possible. The important consideration is that all pupils should have the experience of making the observations as frequently as possible. Many day schools find it very difficult to maintain the records in the holidays or even over the week-end, but this should not deter any teacher from undertaking the work; better to have observations made from Monday to Friday only than not at all. As to the duration, it is probable that, for single daily observations, at least a term is necessary for real benefit to be derived; more desirable is a whole year.

The kind of practical work just described has as its essential purposes the understanding by the pupils of how to read the instruments, the significance of the units, the range of the main elements, the provision of basic information in preparation for more advanced work later, and the practical demonstration that geography is concerned with real things. But something more is possible and very desirable. As suggested in another connexion, one of the main considerations in modern geography is the study of relationships, and this is as important in weather study as it is in respect of surface features of the earth. Relationship between the elements cannot be demonstrated effectively if the observations are taken only once a day. A more valuable practice would be to initiate *intensive* weather study for a comparatively short period. The procedure is to organize the readings of the elements mentioned above in the normal routine several times during the day, say every two hours, for as much of the daylight as possible, for a continuous period of two or three weeks. More than one class may be involved providing there is easy access to the recording chart. The only divergence from this routine is that the rain-gauge is read only once a day at an agreed time. The advantages will be apparent. British weather changes so rapidly that a daily reading of the elements gives a very imperfect picture of what is really happening. More important, this intensive study makes possible clear demonstration of the close relationship between the elements. The onset of a depression would be marked by increasing cloud and its changing character, the falling barometer, possibly by changes in temperature and wind direction and force, and probably by the incidence of rain. The significance of warm and cold fronts may take on a new meaning and have more reality than that provided by the daily set of readings or the oral description. It is true, however, that striking changes of temperature at ground level often do not occur as fronts pass, and many depressions crossing Britain are wholly or partly occluded. In addition this system permits more effective comparison with the published weather maps, which can be usefully displayed alongside the recording chart. There are practical advantages too. Many teachers have found that it requires real effort to keep all the individuals of a class in the state of sustained interest which is necessary to ensure a complete record over the long period required if the readings are made once in twenty-four hours. On the other hand, interest can be easily maintained for the few weeks of the intensive system, and only one or two week-ends call for volunteers. Adjustment of the length of the period ensures, also, that individuals shall have as much observing practice as under the normal system.

Beyond the immediate impacts stressed above, some form of weather record is very necessary for secondary pupils, in connexion with climatic aspects of their regional work. The benefits of dealing intimately with local weather can bring greater reality to the climates the pupil only hears or reads about. A temperature of 60° F. in the shade or 100° F. in the sun has real significance to the pupil who has made these observations several times; actual experience with the rain-gauge can make the observer appreciate what a lot of rain has to fall to make up an inch of rainfall. In other words, weather observations provide a standard to help the pupil to imagine more accurately weather conditions in other parts of the world and thus the realities that lie behind the generalizations called "climate." In the main the pupil in school is brought up on an unrelieved diet of *average* climatic statistics; acquaintance with actual readings can help to apply a corrective. Averages have their place but pupils should have brought to their notice the much greater, real significance of the actual conditions. Just as they themselves have been affected by the heavy fall of snow, the low temperature of an early morning which glazes the roads, the migration of the school out-of-doors when the temperature topped the eighties, so they should appreciate that it is the actual climatic conditions—that is, the weather—which affect the lives and livelihoods of people in other lands. When averages are given it would be well to indicate the actual temperature and rainfall which a region is likely to experience at different seasons. As Professor A. A. Miller says, "Weather is a reality that can be observed and is appreciated by the observer; climate is an abstraction, a confusion of figures of each element divorced from and unrelated to the others though everybody observes that they occur together." [1]

For pupils following more advanced courses practical weather study provides a sound introduction to the better understanding of the official weather map and to the conception of air-mass climatology. Some teachers and pupils might be interested in the possibility of the exchange of meteorological information between schools in different parts of the country. For a time an organization was in existence which facilitated this. [2]

The influence of such local features as relief, aspect, and soil on the weather is very marked; places separated by only a few miles may have quite different records. [3] The dip and scarp slopes of the Chilterns may show differences of 5° F., while in the same area a hill station may have five inches of rain more a year than a place in the valley below. Even in large urban areas climatic conditions vary from one part to another to a surprising degree. In London, for example, at Hampstead, 410 feet above sea level, the average rainfall is nearly two inches a year more than at Camden Square, two miles away and 300 feet lower. Average temperatures are also lower at the former station. There is no doubt that the artificial surface of a town with its tarred or concrete streets, its pavements, and its buildings of varying height influence strongly some elements of the weather, especially temperature and fog. Pioneer work might well be done by pupils in urban schools in mapping the distributions of temperature under different conditions in the streets surrounding the school. Much research on the whole subject of micro-climates has already been

[1] *Geography*, Vol. XXXVIII, p. 58 (April 1953).
[2] See *Geography*, Vol. XXXIX, p. 182 (July 1954).
[3] Meteorological data for near-by stations may be obtained from tables of statistics published by the Meteorological Office at the Air Ministry.

undertaken, but much remains to be done, and weather records in both urban and rural schools might help in this important work.

The practical activities described briefly in this chapter are capable of considerable variation and extension. Not only do they demonstrate that geography is concerned with concrete aspects of the environment but they also provide valuable opportunities for correlation with other subjects of the curriculum in ways elaborated in a later chapter.

# 7

## The Right Use of Large-scale Maps

IT should not be necessary to emphasize the importance of maps as the geographer's unique method of expression or the importance of teaching pupils to read and make good use of large-scale maps. Quite apart from their value in relation to geographical study, the ability to use a topographical map is something which can bring lasting pleasure, and has a continuing value to anyone whose interests extend beyond his own back garden. While it is true that from time to time the geographer has to make maps, particularly sketch-maps, it is of more fundamental importance that he should be able to use maps: so much of what he may want to record in cartographical form will be recorded on the base of published maps, and so much of what he wants to know will be found on a large-scale map, which in a sense begins to do the geographer's job for him by showing the place relationship of a fair variety of facts of human and physical geography.

Even a good large-scale map has its limitations, as some of the suggestions already made regarding activities which can profitably be carried out in the field, have indicated. Nevertheless, for most parts of the country, and certainly of other countries, we have to rely upon secondhand sources and among these maps and pictures are very important.

In considering here the use of maps and not the making of maps, we do not overlook the fact that there may be a place in the school curriculum for some simple introduction to surveying. This, in a sense, is another type of field-work in which geography and mathematics go together, and we have seen some rather exciting work by boys of average ability in simple surveying. In one case at least this came out of the mathematics time and not the geography time, and it may be that the geography teacher would find it difficult to give sufficient time to survey to make much of it. (Further reference is made to this matter in Chapter 9, p. 106.) Whether or not surveying can be found a place, let it be said at this stage that we ought not to expect pupils to be able to make maps of any degree of accuracy and value without either a proper simple survey or an accurate published map on which to base their efforts. To expect, for example, a class of twelve-year-olds to make, unaided, a map of their routes to school seems to us to demand something which the teacher himself might find unreasonably difficult.

In teaching pupils to read maps we would emphasize *using* maps as the best approach, for, in this way, learning about the shorthand of conventional signs and relief representation is linked up with a sense of purpose in that the map is being referred to in order to find out something about the country which it shows. When a form of eleven-year-olds comes to their first geography lesson in their new secondary school there could probably be no better start to their geography at this new stage in their education than for the teacher to give to each pair of pupils a copy of the 6-in. or $2\frac{1}{2}$-in. sheet, which includes the school itself, and to leave the pupils to look at it for themselves, uninterrupted by any class-teaching, for some fair period of time. The interested buzz as the pupils find where they live, where the school is, and other features already known to them, is a rewarding sound, and individuals will ask questions, and the teacher can begin to make personal contact with this new class by talking to the boys or girls as they look at this large-scale map. We have found it helpful to follow this first opportunity for the pupils to use a map for themselves by giving them one or two imaginary journeys within the compass of the map. The teacher may make sure that everyone has located the school, and then describe a route to be taken step by step, the pupils following it on the map (here, perhaps, the value of supplying only one map between two may be emphasized since it reduces the number of pupils who get lost on the way), and, having turned to the left and taken the second on the right and followed this footpath or that, he will then ask where the class has arrived, and find out how many have not been able to follow. This imaginary kind of journey on the map will then be undertaken in different surroundings, perhaps in those many cases where the school is in an urban area by going out to the countryside and imagining a journey through more open country, and gradually questions will call for observation of what information the map is giving about the countryside, which will lead to the interpretation of the conventional signs, including those employed to show relief.

We are strongly opposed to teaching the conventional signs divorced from the use of a map. The way to learn to read a map is like the modern way of learning to read—that is, by "look-and-say" methods. It is unrealistic, and indeed unnecessary, to put on the board a long list of conventional signs to be carefully copied, and *after that* to hand out the maps. Far better to use the maps imaginatively and, if possible, amusingly (on the country walk, for example, we may remark that "So-and-so appears to have got left behind at this point," and "how has that come about?"), and we shall find that the interpretation of the conventional signs comes naturally and easily. After some of them have been used and interpreted more than once, *then* it may be suitable for each pupil to make a note of the signs already identified, adding to his list as experience grows.

This policy may be acceptable, and indeed is often employed, in respect of the conventional signs; but when we come to contours we have found that many teachers feel it necessary to teach about contours directly and unrelated to the use of a large-scale topographical map before attempting to interpret them on the map itself. We would plead that at least the experiment should be tried of building up an understanding of the significance of contours in relation to the use of maps before starting to make those oval-shaped islands so much favoured in early textbooks. We have, for example, in carrying out an imaginary journey on a 1-in. map with a class of girls labelled "backward," asked, "Are we going uphill or down?" and had the answer, "Uphill." "How do you know?" "Because of the orange lines"—and whether or not at this stage they are called contours, these same youngsters, whose ability may be so ill-thought of, readily reached the conclusion on their own that where the orange lines were closer together the slope was steeper. This is a first step towards using the contours of the map to find out what the country is like, and the simpler land forms can gradually be identified. But let it be remembered that for many children in a large city the term "valley" means little or nothing, and to draw the V-shaped contours of a valley on the blackboard, to have them copied and labelled "valley," may be completely unrealistic. But to walk across, in imagination, a piece of countryside, and to find that we go downhill to the river, cross the river, and then go uphill, may be more realistic, and from this experience, repeated and extended, may be built up both a realistic conception of a valley and a real appreciation of the shapes of the contours which identify it on the map. A hill is easier than a valley to deal with in the geography-room. Its shape is known and when its contour pattern is found on the large-scale map it is readily identified by almost all children without their needing to be told first. The experience of hill and valley forms gained in this way must certainly be confirmed in varied ways which will include oblique aerial photographs and notebook-copying of some of the contour forms and perhaps modelling. Ideally we would add the building up of landscape in the sand-tray from the information given by a large-scale map.

None of this, of course, is really a proper substitute for the experience of crossing a valley or climbing a hill, out-of-doors, in person, map in hand. The best way to teach the understanding of contours is by comparing the map and the ground on the spot. The first step in map-use out-of-doors is to set the map. "I am here on the map, the church is there; so I point the line from me on the map to the church on the map towards the church I can see." It may not be easy for pupils to visualize the position on sloping ground of a horizontal line. We may therefore spread out the pupils across a slope so that they are all at the same height, each checking his neighbour by the simplest of home-made clinometers or levels. The pupils are then along what is discovered to be a contour, and are making a line the shape of which is found to be on the map. Other ways of learning to read a map by using it out-of-doors have already been referred to in an earlier chapter (p. 32).

This ground work of the use of maps, and the gradual building up of the ability to read them, should lay the foundation for the continuing use of large-scale maps on a number of occasions throughout the geography course. The geography-room ought to become in the minds of the pupils a kind of laboratory, well stocked with large-scale maps, to which it is natural to refer individually or in groups on many occasions and as required, and the teacher will no doubt aim at being in a position to be able to say to a boy or a girl, "Go to such and such a map-drawer, such and such a file of pictures or film-strip or book, and find out for yourself."

There is a real danger and disadvantage at any stage in too much teaching of map-reading divorced from any sense of purpose in relation to the broader field of geographical study as a whole, and the pattern of work which we unfortunately sometimes descend to, particularly if our pupils are preparing for a public examination, in which we stop "doing" South America and start "doing" Ordnance Survey maps for a fortnight, is very regrettable. If large-scale maps have been continually and properly used throughout the course it will never be necessary to "do" Ordnance Survey maps at all.

We would particularly emphasize the value of approaching regional study through the large-scale map. It is far more realistic to begin a study of the South Wales valleys by finding out all that we can about them from a 1-in. Ordnance Survey extract than to begin with the small-scale atlas map, and indeed on the extract for this area published by the Geographical Association almost all the significant features of the geography of these coalmining valleys can be identified. It remains to generalize from these details to the broader area, to identify the limits of the coalfield on a smaller-scale map, to deal with industries and so on, but in starting large-scale, particularly if pictures can be associated with the map, we have done two most valuable things—namely, started realistically, and taken some further steps in the right use of large-scale maps. Almost any region of the British Isles can be approached in this way provided the teacher has had the opportunity to collect a set of large-scale map extracts relating to it. If with the use of single copies of large-scale foreign maps in the episcope this can be extended to at least some other parts of the world there is a similar value in realism and some interesting introduction to variations in cartographical method.

In addition to the value of the large-scale map as a start on a region we may suggest the importance of approaching topics of physical geography in the same sort of way. The best way to begin to deal with glaciation, surely, is to use the Ordnance Survey map of, say, part of North Wales, to discover many of the particular physical features which will then be explained in terms of past glaciation. We may refer back at this point to the importance of a proper appreciation of slope. We need hardly describe the kind of exercises, for example, in cross-section drawing which will help to bring out the salient features of a glaciated mountain landscape, but we may plead once again for the use of a true vertical scale so that the pupils realize, for example, that the sides of a so-called U-shaped valley are very far from vertical. The continual use of the large-scale map seems to us one of the best ways of ensuring that the teaching of physical geography is not merely theoretical. How much better to find out about a particular river from accurately recorded information about it than to begin with a hypothetical block diagram, and then search the map, or, still worse, the atlas, for examples to fit in with it.

It is at a fairly late stage that pupils may attempt some true interpretation of the geography of an area from the published large-scale maps. Let it be clear that, as has been said in a preceding chapter, there are necessarily limitations to the extent to which this is possible, and let us add that the task is quite a difficult one. It is easy for a teacher almost unconsciously to bring to bear upon the interpretation of a particular map extract quite a lot of geographical knowledge of the area which he may have and which the pupils do not possess, and we should expect pupils of average ability to need a good deal of help in interpreting the countryside from the map as distinct from reading the map to find out about it. Nevertheless, the large-scale map does give a valid opportunity for the pupils to look for correlations between different geographical facts, provided the danger of assuming that because two things occur in the same place they are necessarily causally related is not overlooked.

One final suggestion may be made. In the geography-room there will be plenty of display space, and we would urge that in building up a particular display the large-scale map should often be used. Records, for example, of the expedition or the school journey in the form of photographs and sketches should usually be displayed in association with the large-scale map, which will identify their location, and it is a valuable and interesting piece of work to give to a group to invite them to arrange the display of the material and, by coloured threads or some such means, to link the pictures and sketches and even verbal descriptions with the correct points on the map which we would expect would have been used at the time.

# 8

## Group Learning and Teaching

SOMETHING has been said in earlier chapters about the general educational value of group activities in encouraging a sense of co-operation and team-work, and examples have been given of group work which can be carried on out-of-doors. There is equally an important place for group activities in the geography-room itself. We may consider the place which they have first of all in relation to the work for which the responsibility is placed upon the pupils themselves, although later we shall wish to consider their value as units for direct teaching. It is clear that there is great value in giving to children a sense of exploration and discovery in their work in geography and placing upon them the responsibility for finding out for themselves as much indoors as out-of-doors. Too often, in our view, this giving of the pupils the responsibility for finding out is organized so that each pupil is expected individually to find out the same information as each of the other pupils, and the pattern of work becomes one in which either all the pupils are being taught the same thing at the same time directly, or told to do the same thing at the same time individually. Neither of these forms of activity in the geography-room is itself mistaken, but we are of the opinion that the third element in the pattern of the organization of teaching and learning—namely, that of the group—is of at least equal importance.

In the matter of finding out for themselves the arrangement

of the pupils into groups or teams of, say, four or six each has some practical advantages. A group, by co-operative effort, can go further and achieve a more worthwhile result than an individual working alone, and by giving different responsibilities to each of the groups a wider field can be covered by the class as a whole, and the salient points arising from the work of each group passed on subsequently in one or more of several different ways to the whole class.

Before we consider some examples of the kind of work which may properly be done in this way, it will be wise to indicate a fundamental conception of the place of sheer factual knowledge in the geography course which underlies our thinking about the content of the syllabus. It is that the factual content possible in a geography course may be thought of as consisting of two areas of information. The core area covers that minimum of factual knowledge in geography which we would feel the pupils should really carry away with them from any particular year's work. Around and outside this core is a much larger area of factual knowledge, all of which is sufficiently significant to be worth while but which is too large to be covered, at any rate by all the pupils. About this wider area of knowledge, therefore, two things may be said. First, that within it there is obviously the opportunity for choice of one piece of study rather than another—a choice which will often be made by the teacher but which should sometimes be made by the pupils themselves; and, secondly, that much of the ground covered in work relating to this area of factual knowledge will provide the pupils with background, will enrich their experience, and will be dealing with facts which, if met again, will be recognized or recalled, but which we would not necessarily expect every pupil to remember. It is within this area of geographical study that the opportunity arises in applying the syllabus to any particular group of pupils to ensure that the more able groups cover more ground and carry away more information, and that the less able groups are expected to cover less ground and to carry away rather less information.

Beyond this second area is a vast amount of information which may have geographical relevance but which is not sufficiently significant to secondary-school pupils of the particular age group to be worth while including in the geography course. One of the dangers against which we must safeguard is that individual or group investigation may easily lead pupils into this area of information which, while not strictly irrelevant, is of insufficient significance, and it is a very real danger of some social-studies courses that too much time appears to be taken up finding out too much about too little. In a good geography course we cannot afford to let this happen.

Group work, in which the responsibility for finding out information is placed upon the team, will usually cover ground within the second area described. It will therefore generally be suitable for each group in a form to be given a different subject, and for the groups to have some choice of subject. The lines of investigation will need to be discussed, and the sources of information to be prepared so that, as far as possible, the work of each group does not stray very far into the third area but, on the contrary, has a clearly understood relationship to the core area of factual knowledge, which may very well have been the subject of class-teaching, of individual learning and testing. Perhaps an example will serve to make the matter clearer. Let us suppose that the class is concerned with south-western England. The core area of factual information would probably be fairly rapidly agreed among geography teachers, and, beside a minimum of place-name recognition, would include a few basic facts of physical and human geography. Beyond this there may be, perhaps, half a dozen subjects of interest about which further details can be discovered which are relevant and interesting and lie within the second area of fact. We have in mind, for example, the china-clay industry, fishing, the tourist industry, the production of early flowers and vegetables, and a more detailed study of one or two smaller regions within the large region such as Dartmoor, the Vale of Taunton, and the Bristol area. Provided that sources of information by way of large-scale maps, pictures, and geography-room library books are available to the groups, in such a way that they will have rapid access to them, it is quite possible for a group within one lesson to get together some interesting details which may be passed on to the class as a whole at the next lesson. This reporting to the class as a whole may be done orally, but if this is so it should become apparent to the pupils by experience that such oral reporting of geographical information necessarily calls for some visual expression in addition. Equally some of the groups may in effect report entirely through the miniature exhibition of maps, pictures, written paragraphs, and possibly specimens. Let it be emphasized, however, that, in so far as the reports are made in this way, it is very important to arrange sufficient time for the remainder of the class to study the displays. Occasionally we feel such displays, particularly at the back of the room, face the appreciative eye of the teacher and the visitor, but are virtually unseen by the class.

Such methods are probably already familiar to most teachers. We would add, however, the value of the group as a direct teaching unit, which is perhaps rather more often overlooked in the secondary school. It is by now commonplace among our primary-school colleagues that much of the direct teaching—for example, of reading and number—is most economically done neither with forty children at once nor with one child at a time, but with a group of six or eight children. Too often in the secondary schools, however, we tend to assume—perhaps because there has been selection of children for the school or, more particularly, because the class is streamed—that it is appropriate to teach the whole class all at once and to test the children individually on what they have learnt from such direct teaching. It may be that this is reasonably effective, but where the direct teaching involves oral question and answer it is clear that while one boy or girl is answering the remainder of the class may not be fully participating or, at least, is not learning. If, for example, as part of our core of minimum factual knowledge we want to make sure that each individual in the class really knows the location of half a dozen places in South-west England, we should do it best, if we could, by drilling each child individually. This we cannot do. If, however, we drill the class as a whole the chances are that at the end there will be a number of individuals who will be uncertain of at least one or two of the half-dozen places. Most geography teachers, having recently set a written test, would probably admit, at least to themselves, that this is the case. Should we not therefore be more likely to get a successful result within the time at our disposal if we could drill six or eight children at a time? The element of competition to answer remains but the opportunity of picking out individual uncertainty is far greater. It is by no means impossible to transfer this responsibility to the leader of a group, and a pattern of learning that is both stimulating and effective is that in which the group learn together the factual information on, say, a sketch-map, and then each individual is orally tested upon it by the leader of the group. Such an activity can readily form one of the items of group work in a group teaching lesson which we shall go on to describe.

The kind of lesson which we have in mind is one which some teachers may find novel but which, in our experience, is unusually stimulating to the pupils though at the same time somewhat exacting for the teacher. We would not advocate this kind of lesson more often than, say, three or four times in a term, but it is because of the unusual stimulus to the children which we have found that it gives that we would urge teachers to experiment with it from time to time. Let us suppose that the class is divided into half a dozen groups, each with its own group leader. We shall then arrange for six different items of group work to be ready in different parts of the geography-room, each of them relating to the particular part of the syllabus under consideration at the time, and prepared in such a way that the essence of each job can be done within about seven minutes. It is to be hoped, therefore, that during the course of the lesson each group will have the opportunity of tackling each of the six pieces of work in succession though, of course, it is very possible to spread the activity over a double period or to allow that each group will tackle less than the complete set of activities or that the number may be completed at a succeeding lesson. However, one of the important aspects of this particular technique is the stimulus to the pupils which comes from a sense of urgency, a sense that a particular job has got to be done within a short time, and the kind of reward which the teacher may receive for the trouble taken to arrange a lesson of this kind, may be the sort of remark heard on a recent occasion from a girl in a class of very average ability who, at the end of forty minutes, asserted that she had never worked so hard in her life.

It will be best, perhaps, to give examples of the kind of group tasks which have proved successful within the limits of the pattern proposed, always allowing that the teacher will, of course, in practice make up his own list, will learn from experience, and will arrive at a pattern which suits his own circumstances and may very well be different from that proposed here. Our own list would be somewhat as follows :

(1)    Film strip—the group leader goes through an agreed small number of frames on a film strip shown by rear projection, the object of the group being to identify each picture as it is seen, and then, on going through the frames again, to write down individually the items seen with the area to which they relate. The teacher will visit this particular group as they begin work to make sure that the leader operates the strip projector

correctly, to give the number of frames to be viewed, and the instruction described above. Possibly on a second fleeting visit he will check that the recognition of the one or two more difficult pictures has been correct.

(2) On a blackboard laid horizontally on a couple of geography-tables an outline of the area being dealt with has been drawn, and on it placed half a dozen specimens of the products of the area, each in the particular part of it from which the product especially comes. The pupils at this second task will examine the products, decide what each of the products is, and then name the area from which it comes, if possible with reasons. This identification and the additional details can be noted by the children if time permits. On a later occasion the teacher will make sure that all the specimens have been correctly identified or give the answer to those which remain unknown.

(3) The remaining groups of work must be such that the pupils can get started without immediate help from the teacher, and in each case, therefore, some instructions written up, usually in the form of questions to be answered from data provided, will be necessary. The third group, for example, may come to three or four large pictures relating to some particular geographical aspect of the area being considered and will have to find out the answers to questions written up on the adjoining blackboard from the pictures themselves. (Further reference is made to the use of pictures in Chapter 10, p. 120.) We have found it an advantage to give to the whole class general instructions before the lesson gets going, and to stress that in every case the team has first of all to discuss and agree upon the answers to the problems given, and that not until that has been done should the individuals write down questions and answers. Indeed, we do not attach particular importance to the written results of a lesson of this kind but see its particular value rather in the

team-work investigation and the decision upon agreed solutions.

(4) Three or four wall charts of the kind which have been increasingly produced in recent years will similarly provide information from which the answers to questions written up beside them can be ferreted out, and the procedure of the group will be similar to that described under (3). In each of these cases, of course, the teacher will visit the group as often as he can, making sure that they are not completely held up by some unforeseen difficulty, and checking that in general the conclusions they are reaching are along the right lines. The responsibility of the group leader, both in getting the agreed answers from the contributions of individuals in the team and being able quickly to tell the teacher how far the group has got, is an important one.

(5) Similar use may be made of a straightforward map. We have found it successful for this to be a small-scale wall-map, the questions picking up simple points as to distances and position, relief and communications. Equally successful is the use of a large-scale map by the group in the kind of way described in the preceding chapter.

(6) The last item of group work can very suitably be the straightforward test map described above. We have found that the responsibility placed on the group leader to make sure within a space of a few minutes that the answers to, say, ten numbered places or facts on the test map are not only agreed but known by each individual in the group is usually very effectively carried out.

In planning the half-dozen or so items of work in relation to the point reached in the syllabus, it is generally a good idea to make sure that one or two of them are in effect revision of work done, one or two—for example, the pictures or the wall charts—an extension of topics recently touched upon, and perhaps one or two reaching out to ground not yet covered by the class and thus beginning new work on the very sound basis of group investigation by the children themselves.

The key factors in the success of a lesson of this kind would seem to us to be, first, careful preparation of the jobs of work —this, in our experience, takes about twenty minutes—second, the speed at which the whole lesson moves, and third, the supreme importance of the minute injection of direct teaching into the work of each group at each job of work. While such a lesson is obviously more easily arranged in a good-sized geography-room, let it not be supposed that it is impossible in an ordinary classroom, for our experience is to the contrary. Nevertheless, if space is very limited or if the novelty of the plan a little alarming at first there is no reason at all why the principles of this kind of lesson should not be applied by providing opportunities, say, for three jobs of work to be done in this way by each of six groups within the same time limits, thus ensuring that half the class at any rate is, we hope, peacefully seated and quietly occupied all the time.

# 9

## Practical Work in Geography

PREVIOUS chapters have stressed that pupils of all ages learn geography best by *doing* things and by finding out things for themselves—participating in a directed walk in the country with specific questions to answer, attempting to sketch landscape features from a given viewpoint, investigating the immediate locality of the school, planning tours with the aid of Ordnance Survey maps, solving problems using maps and corresponding pictures, and so on. All of these things involve mental activity, and some of them physical activity as well. So far, in speaking of group and individual work, we have made little reference to practical work in the narrower sense of the term. Many pupils, including the younger and also the less able, appreciate and benefit from as much physically active work in the classroom as possible. What forms can this take? In the geography course, the making of models holds an important place. Simple model-making need not consume a great deal of time nor demand large supplies of expensive material, especially if the work is planned on co-operative lines so that all members of the class contribute something towards a single, large model.

Suppose that lessons have been taken on aspects of North Africa: then the pupils might combine to produce a large model of an oasis town. Discussion with the class will establish the main features which ought to be illustrated—the pool, the irrigation channels, the rows of crops, the date palms, the buildings, the roads, the arid surroundings, and so on. The items will then be distributed amongst the pupils, a few will make the trees, others the houses, a pair will be responsible for the preparation of the "ground" and, in consultation with the teacher, the superficial distribution of the features. All groups will make full use of pictures in order to have an accurate idea of the appearance of the items they are going to contribute.

Such a scheme stimulates interest, especially among the younger and the slower pupils, it helps to consolidate the material taught and make it more real, it provides opportunity for the application of practical skills in the handling of various media, and above all it ensures valuable training in co-operation—a demonstration of the benefits to be derived from working in groups for the attainment of a common end. Naturally no teacher would embark on such work without careful preparation, not only by thinking out the features to be represented and the materials needed, but also in the training of the pupils to work together in groups. The need for progression here is as great as in any part of school work. It would be the height of folly to embark on an elaborate group model unless pupils had been prepared by simple exercises beforehand. The first stage in training might involve the whole class making the same simple model under the direction of the teacher; in the second the class would be divided into two sections with one half making a development of the first model on their own while the other tackled a new one. The third stage would involve smaller groups and training in more independent working. Ultimately the class will learn to do things with a minimum of fuss, and pupils will come to rely on their own judgments and experience. Each small group should have a leader, who needs to have some measure of control over the activity of each member, and who alone of the group should make contact with the teacher.

At this stage a few words on materials may be helpful. It is essential to have a firm surface on which to build the model. If the construction can take place on an old card-covered table which can remain in the classroom throughout the duration of the work there is no difficulty. Frequently, however, the model has to be moved at the end of the lesson and in these circumstances a firm base is essential. Compressed fibre board or hardboard is very suitable; a piece of appropriate size can be purchased for a few shillings, and it can be retained as the base for subsequent models.

Varying textures for the representation of fairly flat landscapes can be made with a thin mixture of superfine plaster of Paris (dental plaster) and water tinted with powder-colour brushed over the surface and allowed to dry. Variation in effect can be secured by the addition of small quantities of size or sawdust to the original mixture. Papiermâché may be used for the same purpose, but unless very thin the substance takes long in drying and may cause warping of its support. Undulating landscapes are best made from sacking brushed over thoroughly with hot, thin glue and spread over bunched-up newspaper. While it is still pliable the glued hessian with the paper below can be pushed into any desired form, the U-shaped valley, the escarpment, or the incised plateau, and, quickly drying, will retain that shape and present a very hard surface which may be painted as required. Hilly landscapes can also be secured by using strips of paste-covered newspaper woven in and out of shaped wire-netting of wide mesh. The surface can then be painted or pasted again and sprinkled with sawdust or powdered chalk.

Space will not permit a full discussion of the many possibilities in the use of common materials for the representation of human and natural features. Empty cartons, matches and their boxes, raffia, sisal string, pipe-cleaners, shredded loofah, corrugated cardboard, wire, sponge, cotton wool, milk straws, and cotton all have their uses. Surprisingly realistic effects may be secured by encouraging pupils to experiment on lines suggested by the teacher.

With profit the sand-tray might be used more often for providing the base for such group models. If the proper zinc-lined tray is not available a drawer out of a plan-press does admirably. The sand may be moulded to represent any minor feature of the landscape, such as a shallow depression, a broad valley, or a line of low hills, and it can be tinted by scraping coloured chalk or sprinkling powder-colour over it. The sand provides an excellent medium for supporting model trees, fences, buildings, etc. It is clean, cheap, and can be used many times.

Some teachers have found that a useful form of practical activity is the making of a diorama which can be on show as a semi-permanent form of illustration in the geography-room. Silhouettes of landscape features, vegetation, animals, and people arranged to stand at appropriate distances from a suitable "back-cloth" can give an effect of depth which is valuable. Sets of coloured prints for dioramas with suggestions for making and arrangement may be obtained from the Commonwealth Institute at South Kensington.

The organization and technique suggested above may be used in the making of a group model to illustrate features of the school locality. For some pupils the relationship between the landscape and the human use of it, either rural or urban, becomes more real if it is translated from the two-dimensional map into the three-dimensional model. This form of activity calls for more accuracy than the model illustrating some distant scene; the map must be read and measured with great care, and there must not be undue exaggeration of the vertical scale. Such a model is valuable in connection with school-journeys or camps held at a fixed centre. Pupils will be better prepared to follow the map and recognize salient features of the new environment if they have already studied the 1 : 25,000 map for the purpose of making a model, and many will profit from its use at the school journey centre.

These locality models raise the question of the most suitable method of showing relief. Papiermâché can be shaped with ease and some accuracy. There are several modelling substances in addition to "Plasticine," used with or without wooden pegs set vertically as guides to indicate exact height, which can give good results, but probably the easiest and most accurate method is to use sheets of card thin enough to be cut easily with scissors or razor-blade. Contours of the required area are first traced, preferably from the 1 : 25,000 Ordnance Survey map, and enlarged to suitable size by any of the usual methods; the episcope can be used very effectively for this. The vertical interval of this map is twenty-five feet, but an extra contour can be interpolated if desired. The contours are then traced on to the card, a pair of adjacent contours to each sheet. The lower contour is cut out, the upper one provides a guide for the accurate positioning of the next sheet after it has been cut. A good adhesive and pressure will ensure that the sheets stick firmly, but the whole should be fastened to a stout base such as a sheet of hardboard or three-ply to prevent warping. A thin wash of superfine plaster of Paris will smooth the contours, and after it is dry it may be painted to show any desired distribution. It seems a pity to colour such a model simply by height, for by its nature it already shows relief.

The vertical scale should not exceed five times the horizontal so the thickness of the card must first be measured; this is most accurately done by measuring the thickness of, say, ten sheets and working a simple division sum. Occasionally there is room for the model made by teacher or pupil to elucidate a concept which the class may find difficult. Many pupils, for example, have difficulty in understanding a description of something involving three dimensions when only the two-dimensional blackboard is available for illustration. The layout of shafts, roadways, and galleries in a coalmine and their relationship to the working face and to the surface is made much more readily comprehensible if a simple model is constructed in a large grocer's carton. The container, turned on its side, with the open top facing the class, would display layers of card representing seams worked at different levels, cut back to varying distances to show roads and passages and the relationship with the shaft and the pit-headgear which is represented on the top.

Similar simple models might be made to show the form of valleys in a glaciated landscape or the essential features of the layout of a grain elevator or a hydro-electric plant or even of the operation of the purse-seine in fishing. Time spent in this way is repaid by more rapid understanding by pupils and increased interest.

Sometimes the simple model which *works—e.g.*, a canal lock —can prove an invaluable teaching aid. Irrigation devices such as the shaduf or the tambour can be made much more real and comprehensible if methods of using them can be demonstrated concretely although in miniature. Care should be taken to give the pupils an idea of the scale of the model perhaps by indicating the size of the worker. Occasionally some aspect of the work in class may inspire a pupil to construct a model or a working diagram on his own; the movement of wind and pressure belts in subtropical latitudes, the relationship between altitude, climate, and vegetation in the Andes, and the dependence of insolation on the angle of incidence of the sun's rays, are some of the subjects which have been successfully tackled.

Many teachers are inclined to condemn model-making in school out of hand as a glaring example of "eyewash"; they look on it as a form of activity artificially stimulated to provide concrete evidence for the edification and pacification of inspectors. No doubt unrestricted model-making is time-consuming and unjustifiable, but if a reasonable balance is maintained between this and other aspects of the work it has an important part to play especially in classes unfettered by an external examination. Those teachers who have introduced group model-making into some part of their courses have been surprised at the recrudescence of interest which has resulted, and they have been in no doubt as to the success which can be attendant upon this approach. Evidence of this is found in the way in which keen groups will work on their models out of school time—for example, during the lunch hour.

Most geography teachers consider that the amount of time allocated to their subject is quite inadequate, having in mind its wide scope. The shortage of time is sometimes given as the reason for omitting model-making and, more frequently, all aspects of map-making and simple surveying. There is much division of opinion as to the desirability of introducing survey-ing into the geography syllabus. The subject may be included in the mathematics scheme, in which case the need is met, but if not the geographer must consider whether he ought to give some of his classes this experience. If a branch of learning is worth while and relevant to everyday life, and has an appeal for certain types of pupils, then there is a case for introducing it into the curriculum. Those pupils who benefit most from practical work and physical activity, whose studies are not tied to an external examination, may find satisfaction through achievement in aspects of surveying.

Only the simpler techniques should be attempted—for ex-ample, the straight line and offsets method of mapping the school field, the plane table, the use of the simple clinometer (perhaps home-made), similar triangles for widths and heights, the prismatic compass used for making a simple plan or a short traverse, and the method of levelling already described. Some would say that the work would founder because some pupils are unable to use a protractor accurately, but their difficulties would be reduced if a Douglas protractor, a circular instrument graduated from $0°$ to $360°$, were employed.

The essence of good geography is variety of method and approach, and the subject is fortunate in that work can take so many varied forms and that many of these in the truest sense of the term involve "activity." We have stressed at a number of points the value of the exploratory sense in geography, and have given a number of examples of ways in which pupils working either individually or in groups should be encouraged to find out things for themselves. There is a place for individual work on particular topics carried on for part of the geography time over perhaps a period of some weeks. This sort of opportunity may be particularly suitable for older boys and girls who have not any examination objective immediately ahead of them. It carries its dangers, however, and it is to these which we would first of all refer. If a youngster of average ability is turned loose upon a fairly large subject he will tend to collect information about it rather than to acquire knowledge of it. We have seen, for example, thick and neatly produced books compiled by individuals upon which many hours have been spent, often peaceful hours in the geography-room, giving the impression to both teacher and visitor of an orderly and active body of children. Yet there has been nothing in some of these books which is either original or personal to their compiler. They are scissors-and-paste books, and though they may look even more impressive if a great deal of what is in them is pen-written, this material, if it has been simply copied out of another book, is an even greater snare and a delusion since so much time has been uselessly occupied in the mere writing of it. Equally, the gay and often attractive scrapbook about some country or other has little value if it is merely a haphazard collection, put together in no sort of order, of any and every sort of picture that has come to hand about any or every part of the country concerned. The trouble about these compilations is that the making of them keeps the pupils quiet, gives them and their teachers the impression that they are profitably employed, and that they make a good show on "open day," but these collections of information are often without significance and often unremembered if the teacher does no more than provide a mass of sources and collect up the books at the end.

We should do well to follow this destructive criticism with some constructive advice, and it would be not that individuals should not spend time in and out of school making books about topics but that the geography teacher should make quite sure that the work of investigation had clearly defined objectives, that it lay within the area of significant factual information, and that whatever was put down was as far as possible personal to the pupil and understood by him. It is probably best, therefore, to expect each pupil to prepare to begin with a plan of campaign having in mind the chapter headings, as it were, of the ultimate result, subject always to modification as the work goes on. On any particular occasion, therefore, the pupil might be expected to be seeking information about some particular aspect of his topic. He should then be expected to record and illustrate this as far as possible without the source of the information in front of him. This may seem hard and difficult for boys and girls of average ability. Nevertheless, we would think of work on these individual-topic books as being founded upon experience in the geography course of the kinds we have already described; experience, for example, as a member of a team responsible for investigating a topic, assembling information about it, and passing on that information, often orally, to the remainder of the class. The individual pupil working on a topic should work as if he were going to be expected to tell the class what he has found out with the help, perhaps, of a few notes, and if instead of this oral expression of his results he is making a book about them it is no more unreasonable to expect him to record his results in writing, sketch-map, and picture, equally with the help of nothing more than some notes derived from the sources which he has used. There is, perhaps, less to be said for originality in the pictorial and cartographic aspects of his record than in the written part. Nevertheless, the training which he will have had in the making of sketch-maps should come out, and he would be expected to make up his own sketch-maps, always, of course, upon an accurately copied base. There is undoubtedly a place for the collection of pictures cut out from magazines, travel leaflets, and the like, but these ought not to figure in the record except in so far as they bear a direct relationship to what has been written. We can all of us probably compare in our minds the sort of textbook in which not only the sketch-maps but the pictures are an integral part of what is also presented in the text with other less worthy books in which the pictures appear to have been pushed in afterwards with only a vague relationship to the text and, in some cases, it would seem, in a belated attempt to liven it up. There is no reason why we should not expect our individual investigators of topics to justify the inclusion of a particular picture at a particular point, or, if this is a little hard and an attractive picture has been found which merits inclusion, at least to ensure that an original caption indicates its relationship to the subject under consideration.

The criticism which we have made of mere compilation applies, of course, as much to the wall display whether by an individual or by a group or even, dare it be said, by a teacher, as it does to the scrapbook or the topic-book. We would stress the value of urging some at least of the individuals studying varied topics to present their material not in a book but in a display, in the same kind of way suggested for the display of the results of group investigation. It may not be out of place to add a comment upon the identification of pictures. We have probably become aware of the differences between what individual children see in any particular pictures, and there is some benefit as well as interest, and perhaps amusement, to be had from giving pupils the opportunity of setting before other pupils small collections of pictures about particular topics, and asking them to identify what is shown. It is often in explaining to others what he himself knows that a pupil, otherwise not very forthcoming, finds his opportunity to develop and to take a more active part in the work than he has done before.

# IO

## Chalk and Talk

THE pendulum of educational progress swings constantly but through arcs of varying amplitude. New ideas, which are sometimes old ones rehabilitated, seized on by some, and applied and advocated with undiscriminating enthusiasm, cease after a time to be acceptable to the main body of informed teaching opinion; the ideas have been defeated by exaggerated claims or by unwise application. The pendulum swings back, older methods become fashionable again, but the regression is reduced; some advance has been accomplished. The wise and conscientious teacher avoids extremes and endeavours to maintain a sane measure of progress. Very little of what has been said so far has referred to class teaching in the ordinary sense, and indeed we shall rightly be thought to favour "activity methods." Activity on the part of the pupils, providing it is mental as well as physical activity, has everything to commend it. Its application came as a welcome relief from rigid control of pupils in the classroom common in the early years of the century when over-large classes made formal teaching essential. But of course all old methods were not wholly bad, and the sensible teacher combines some of the old and well tried with some of the new and experimental to secure a flexible and varied approach.

Some extremists would dispense with oral teaching, but its passing would be a great loss to educational practice. Many adults can recall from their own schooldays the thrill and inspiration which they derived from oral lessons delivered by expert practitioners. Unfortunately, it is also true that many oral lessons, especially in geography, are far from inspiring, and stimulate little interest in their hearers. The lecture is obviously out of place in the classroom of the secondary school, and the oral lesson which always conforms to a set pattern is almost as bad. This is one reason for suggesting the advisability of making less use of the academic approach, which considers every region according to a formal scheme on the lines of "Position," "Relief," "Climate," "Natural Vegetation," and so on. A scheme such as this is systematic, it appeals to the intelligent and the adult because it is logical, and it may be suitable for the most able pupils. Generally it fails with the slower and less able ones, whose interest needs to be captured from the beginning of the lesson by something vivid and realistic, which will often be an aspect of the human activities of the region.

This does not mean that the essential geographical facts and principles must be submerged and perhaps lost in a welter of chatty sociology. The plan of the lesson might approach the following pattern. First, the teacher should decide the few definite, geographical facts which he proposes to introduce into the lesson and which he hopes the pupils will know at its conclusion. Secondly, he will decide what interest-provoking and probably mainly human material he will introduce into the lesson as a means of conveying to the class the basic information he wishes to teach. Thirdly, he will be at pains to arrange the subject-matter in a logical sequence, a narrative, which the pupils can follow easily because each aspect follows logically from its predecessor. It is important that this sequence should begin with something life-size and vivid, and not with something generalized or abstract. Of course the oral work will not last too long—perhaps less than a half of the total length of the lesson—and will be concluded with some form of revision of the fundamental facts which were planned to form the basis of the lesson.

As an example consider a lesson to pupils of twelve years on the growing of cotton in the "Deep South" of the United States. The main geographical facts which the teacher proposes to stress may be:

(1) The nature of the cotton plant.
(2) Its climatic requirements, especially the long growing season and the need for sunshine, warmth, and moisture (demands which could not be met, say, in East Anglia).
(3) The chief producing areas.

The interest-provoking detail may include Negro spirituals, the slave trade, the reason for slavery in America, scenes in the cotton-fields at different times in the year, the homes and food of the workers. No two teachers would choose exactly the same material, for its selection will depend a great deal on the outlook and background of the individual, but planning on these lines is likely to result in greater definition to the lesson, increased interest by the pupils, and improved opportunities for acquiring and remembering facts. The example may serve to illustrate the dual character of the subject-matter of a lesson planned on the suggested lines. The three headings above constitute what might be called the "Reproduction knowledge"—the basic core of the lesson which should be learned by the pupil. The interesting detail forms "Recognition Knowledge"—the details which add verisimilitude, not necessarily to be remembered but which may be recalled if met again. This is the same kind of distinction as was made in Chapter 8, p. 92, applied now to the content of a single lesson.

At this stage it may not be out of place to suggest that the oral lesson has more chance of success if the teacher has the gift of vivid oral description. This applies particularly to the description of human activity which can be less well demonstrated by static pictures. Ability in this direction is undoubtedly associated with strong powers of visual imagery and a good command of English, but skill in this way may be acquired by anybody who makes a conscious effort and who practises the art.

Reference has already been made in Chapter 7 to the use of large-scale maps as an introduction to the study of an area, but in all regional work the region under discussion must be clearly located on the earth's surface. Wall maps are of value for this purpose, and the pupils' atlases should be used constantly during the oral lesson and in individual work. The atlas has many uses—for showing position, for stressing relationships between distributions, for tracing routes and the courses of rivers—but the teacher should never lose sight of the fact that the atlas map is a compromise; the globe must be referred to constantly as a corrective. There *is* a place for the globe which hangs, Sputnik-like, in the geography-room, but of more value to pupils is the globe which can be examined closely and turned, and the globe (or large ball) which can be moved about freely by the teacher when earth movement is under discussion.

An important method of securing realism in regional work is to make use of "sample studies." A feature or a small area typical of a large region, generally embodying some aspect of human activity, is selected to represent the conditions over the whole region. The description of the life on a particular farm near Saskatoon might be made to demonstrate the salient features of the wheat-growing areas of the prairies. The appearance and purposes of the farm buildings would be described to bring out climatic features, the nature of the building material, and the source of the water supply. The life and work of the farmer and his family through the year would serve to emphasize both the contrasts between the seasons and the features of the prairie which favour this form of farming. The transport of the grain from the farm would lead on to the methods of storing and export from Canada. Finally attention would be given to the distribution of farms similar to the one described, and the delimitation of the wheat-growing area. Similarly, the life on a particular sheep-station in New South Wales would represent conditions over a large portion of south-east Australia; the work at a Pennsylvanian coalmine could be representative of the industry in the whole of the State, and the destination of the coal could lead naturally to related industrial development; the characteristics of the flood-plain of the lower Arun, in Sussex, could typify the conditions of similar features elsewhere. The section of the geography course which *begins* with a sample study is applying the sound principle of proceeding from the particular to the general, and gives the advantage of starting with something which is real, life-size, and within the comprehension of pupils of all types.[1] The chief handicap experienced by teachers wishing to apply this approach is the difficulty of finding authentic material in sufficient detail. The Association of Agriculture[2] publishes some excellent broadsheets which give accounts of selected farms at home and abroad. The Geographical Association plans to publish a pamphlet on sample studies. Some Government publications contain useful material, and of course travel literature is an invaluable source.[3]

Variety of approach to a new topic or region is essential. Some would begin the study of Argentina by sketching briefly the main features of its early history—the significance of the name "Argentina" and of "Rio de la Plata," the smuggling of precious metals and stones from the Spanish Andean conquests through the port on the Atlantic, the development of the stopping-place on the overland route at the "oasis" of Tucuman, where mules could be exchanged and allowed to re-

[1] Valuable guidance in the application of the method is given in *Sample Studies; The Development of a Method*, B. S. Roberson and M. Long, *Geography*, Vol. XLI, p. 248, 1956.

[2] 53 Victoria Street, London, S.W.1.

[3] Useful bibliographies are given in the article cited above and in *Handbook for Geography Teachers* (Methuen, 1955), p. 384.

# ARGENTINA        UNITED KINGDOM

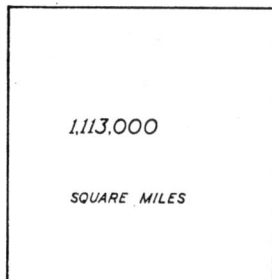

1,113,000

SQUARE MILES

AREA

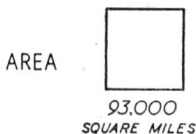

93,000
SQUARE MILES

## POPULATION

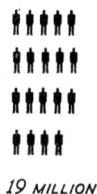

19 MILLION

51 MILLION

## LIVESTOCK

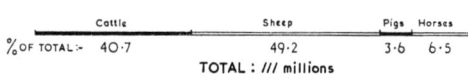

| | Cattle | Sheep | Pigs | Horses |
|---|---|---|---|---|
| % OF TOTAL :- | 40·7 | 49·2 | 3·6 | 6·5 |

TOTAL : 111 millions

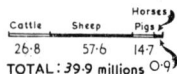

| Cattle | Sheep | Pigs Horses |
|---|---|---|
| 26·8 | 57·6 | 14·7 |

TOTAL : 39·9 millions 0·9

## EXPORTS BY VALUE

**ARGENTINA :-**

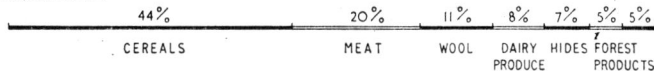

| 44% | 20% | 11% | 8% | 7% | 5% 5% |
|---|---|---|---|---|---|
| CEREALS | MEAT | WOOL | DAIRY PRODUCE | HIDES | FOREST PRODUCTS |

**UNITED KINGDOM:-**

| 6% 4% | 81% | 6% 3% |
|---|---|---|
| FOOD BASIC MATERIALS | MANUFACTURED GOODS | MINERALS FUEL, ETC., |

Fig. 11. A Diagrammatic Approach to the Study of Argentina

cuperate, the mutation of the natives of the plain from hunters on foot to mounted raiders through their capture of escaped Spanish horses, and the gradual extermination of the original inhabitants. The story can be made vivid and logical and can serve to bring out a great deal of valuable geography.

Others might prefer a statistical approach, using diagrams such as are illustrated in Figure 11. Comparison should always be made with Britain, and the diagrams are mainly to stimulate interest, to present a problem, not to provide material for pupils to waste time copying. In the given diagrams attention would be focused on the relative areas of the two nations and the contrast in the sizes of the populations. Possible reasons for the contrast might be considered in relation to the features of land utilization and trade. Some might prefer to start with the population map which demonstrates the concentration of people along the Plate estuary and in the "oases" and the scantiness in south and north; contrasts which require an explanation. Others favour the transect method where imaginary journeys are taken along straight lines radiating from Buenos Aires, each one selected to bring out important features of the landscape and the kind of life which is typical. The display of specimens of maize, wheat, maté, and quebracho can stimulate interest and provide openings for unlimited developments. Variety of approach in regional geography must be the aim.

In geography, as in other subjects, the blackboard provides a very valuable teaching aid for such obvious purposes as the writing up of new terms, making a summary of the lesson, for elucidating difficulties, and for focusing attention by means of quick, simple illustrations. Particularly important is the use of the board for the map or diagram which grows as the lesson proceeds. Take as a simple example the lesson on the position and growth of Rio de Janeiro. The first stage, Figure 12 (a), the drawing of the simplified coastline, may be done before the lesson begins or while the class is engaged on individual tasks, although some teachers would draw the simple shape while the class watches. The discovery by one of the early Portuguese navigators will be mentioned, and his mistake in thinking the great bay was an estuary (Rio). The Sugar Loaf rock will be described and its position marked by a dot. The position of the early settlement can be marked (*b*) as the obvious advantages of the bay as a harbour are discussed. The small town was shut in from the interior by the high edge of the plateau (*c*), but early explorers found a fairly easy route through the mountains, and exploited the agricultural resources of the fertile Parahyba valley (*d*), which also provided a feasible route on to the plateau. The exploitation of the wealth of the interior and the growth of communications (*e*) increased the importance of the port. The population increased to nearly two millions, helping to make the port a great business centre supported by international trade whose salient features may be mentioned (*f*).

The facts selected for emphasis would vary with each teacher, but the method is easy to apply, and has undoubted advantages. It is easy to carry out since the illustration is a sketch-map and is therefore generalized and simplified, yet supplies the detail which is lacking in the school atlas, and which is necessary for the understanding of the subject. The same method is applicable to the diagram which is needed to describe a process or a sequence such as the operation of a blast-furnace or the working of a canal lock. The important feature is that only a few lines or words are added at a time so that exposition and illustration may progress together, and the pupils interest secured and held by appeal to both ear and eye. It is always good to give visual expression to each item of the core—that is, the "reproduction knowledge," as distinct from the "recognition knowledge"—which it is hoped to establish in the pupils' minds.

All teachers would agree on the importance of questioning for securing the co-operation and maintaining the interest of

(a)

(b)

TROPIC

(c)

TROPIC

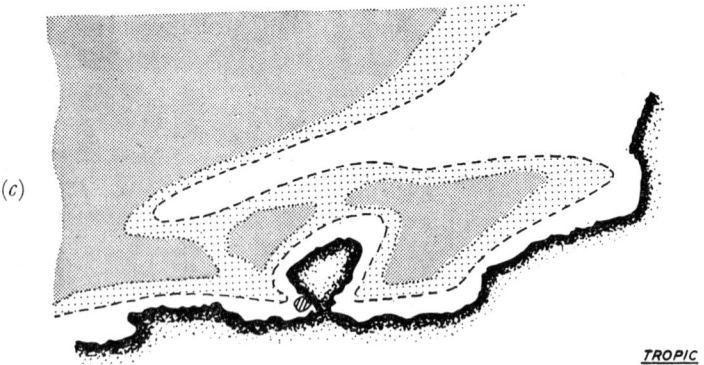

Fig. 12. The Developing Map

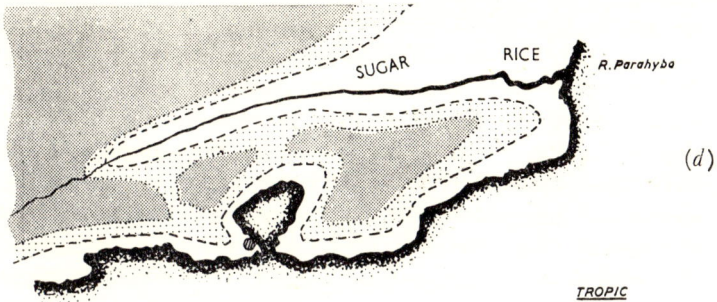

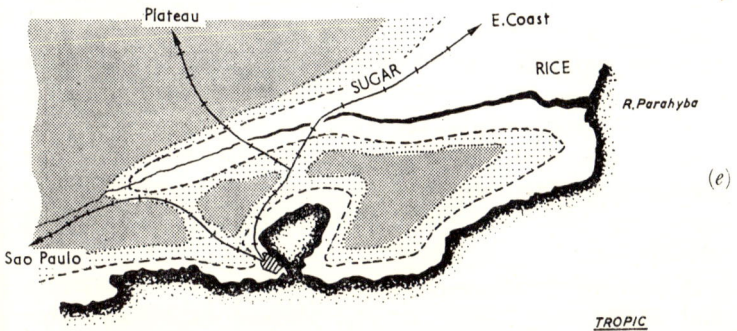

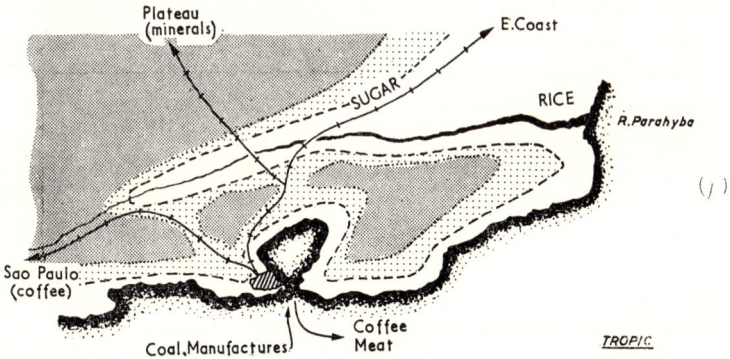

THE DEVELOPING MAP (continued)

the pupils, but questions must be of the right type, and must be introduced at the right place, if they are to be effective. The dramatic effect of a vivid description of some human or animal activity can be spoiled by the introduction of a question just as the climax is being reached. The question should have come well before or immediately after. But this is less serious and more infrequent than the asking of the wrong kind of question. Questions of fact have their place for the revision of past work, for stimulating the laggard, for quelling incipient insubordination, and to ensure understanding, but when the teacher is presenting *new* facts and ideas or old facts in new guises questions should aim at provoking thought. They should be of the type which encourage the pupil to make reasonable deductions from the facts put before him. Through all the work of the school should run the idea that the teacher's essential function is to show pupils how to make the best use of their mental equipment, not merely to provide them with a body of knowledge. Education, not instruction, should be the teacher's primary aim.

A particularly fallacious type of question in geography is that which says, "These are the physical conditions—what crops (or what human activity) would you expect?" This is subtle geographical determinism. Properly we should say, "These are the conditions, these are the crops. How do they relate to one another?"

Pictures of all kinds will greatly enhance the value of the oral lesson, but they must be of the right type, and they must be used purposefully. A picture large enough for the whole class to see clearly provides a useful focus of attention and stimulates interest. It may be used to ensure that children are forming the right concept when they are told for the first time about a new subject—a tropical tree, a strange beast of burden, or a landscape feature. At the same time, through skilful questioning on the lines already suggested, the picture can be used to encourage the pupils to make thoughtful deductions from the features portrayed. A picture (Plate 4, p. 64) of an Australian drover on horseback will illustrate the nature of the country and the characteristics of the vegetation, but it may be used also to lead the pupils to suggest why the horse is necessary, why the shadow beneath the horse is small and very dark, and why the rider wears a broad-brimmed hat.

Similarly, the operation of harrowing may be illustrated by a picture like the one facing page 65 (Plate 5), but pupils may be asked also to describe the vegetation and the nature of the soil and to suggest the state of the weather and the season. The character of the scene may be reminiscent of an English landscape; the fact that the photograph was taken on Long Island may serve as a reminder that New York has only invaded the south-western end.

The techniques described above may be applied to small pictures providing all the pupils can see copies at the same time. An obvious yet much neglected source of small pictures is the pupil's textbook, whose pictures are regarded too frequently as mere embellishments of the book to be hastily scanned and then disregarded. Pupils need to be taught to look at pictures, and to get the most out of them, and the illustrations in the modern textbook, which are usually of a high standard, may be used as real teaching aids.

When a single picture which may be usefully introduced into the lesson is too small to be seen by the whole class it may be passed round either before the lesson begins or when the pupils have started individual work afterwards. It is fatal to encourage the distraction of the pupils' attentions by passing round a picture while oral work continues. If part of the lesson involves the description of something new to the class a picture of it may be passed round before the lesson begins, the teacher first mentioning the essential points needing special attention.

Other ways of using small pictures may be mentioned

briefly. A small number, say eight or ten, may be spaced round the walls of the room for group study. Each picture should have attached to it brief questions requiring short answers in the notebook, or directives for special attention. Each group could have a specified time at each picture before moving on to the next, and it is desirable that during the same period, or as soon after as possible, some of the pupils' work should be considered in class for then the teacher can do much valuable, incidental teaching. A similar technique is possible if there are enough small pictures for individual study. Small pictures may also be projected with the aid of an episcope, but a well-darkened room is essential, and this has its drawbacks.

The film strip has now become part of the standard equipment of most schools, and a few carefully selected frames may be used in the ways suggested above if they are projected so as to present a large, clear picture visible to all. A "daylight" screen with rear projection requires very little darkening of the room, but even front projection on an opaque screen does not need complete darkness. The temptation, of course, is to show the whole strip, once the apparatus is set up and the room prepared, accompanied by a running commentary from the teacher; the old lantern lecture has then returned in new guise, and the class, according to its nature, becomes either somnolent or obstreperous. If the room is only partially darkened the class is able to undertake tasks involving writing or drawing on selected aspects of the pictures displayed.

The ciné film, with its particular property of being able to show movement, has an important part to play in increasing pupils' geographical understanding. This is not the place to examine in detail the techniques of teaching with film, but we may point out that a short film, sound or silent, may introduce a new topic, it may amplify a subject already taken, or it may be used for revision. Whatever the purpose, the discussion which follows the showing is of supreme importance, and when the film is used for teaching new material it is desirable that the film should be short enough to be seen more than once in the lesson. Geography is now well served with a wider selection of good films than any other subject, and the authenticity and interest which this aid provides should encourage teachers who have the apparatus to make full use of it, even if this does entail more careful planning of lessons and encroachment on spare time for the setting up of the apparatus.

The talks arranged by the School Broadcasting Council of the British Broadcasting Corporation give the teacher another valuable means of securing realism, especially when talks are given by people who have had experience in different parts of the world. Some preparation of the pupils beforehand, providing it does not destroy spontaneous interest in the subject, is desirable; follow up with discussion, questions, and exercises is essential. The pamphlets accompanying the talks, which are always well illustrated with pictures and maps, play an important part. Note-taking during the broadcast is an activity best reserved for the older and brighter pupils; others should concentrate on listening. Television is likely to play an increasingly important part in education, but the techniques of use do not differ greatly from those for film and radio, and it cannot in any way take the place of the teacher.

Vegetable and mineral specimens and other objects which may be seen, handled, and perhaps tasted, stimulate much additional interest in the course of the oral lesson. The weightiness of a piece of haematite, the silky texture of the long crystals of chrysotile asbestos, the scent of cloves, the concealment of cotton-seeds in a mass of unginned lint, are valuable teaching aids for they appeal to more than one sense, and they demonstrate that geography is concerned with real if unfamiliar things.

Another approach which can bring interest and a feeling of reality in the oral lesson is the use of carefully selected extracts from travel literature and authentic articles in geographical

magazines. Here is an example from Evelyn Cheeseman's
*Camping Adventures in New Guinea*:

> We scrambled up the yielding scoria [on the slopes of the
> volcano] and stood near the rim of the crater looking down
> into the red fires. It was wonderful to see some of the inner
> machinery exposed to view. There were two blow-holes look-
> ing like huge cauldrons, and a movement underground made
> molten lava in a red-gold liquid pour from the upper to the
> lower. As this was taking place lumps of scoria were falling
> in with the lava from the sides, until the steam inside could
> not get sufficient outlet. Then came an explosion lasting a few
> minutes. What had sounded like thunder when echoing among
> the hills was like a tremendous roar when we looked into the
> vent. Then out shot the rocks which were blocking it several
> hundred feet up into the air, and were caught in the strong
> wind that was blowing, and carried away from us over to
> the opposite slopes. . . .
>
> At the same instant came the next roar and masses of rock
> shot out directly over our heads instead of on the other side.
> We had no time to run round the rim, for bits of small rock
> were already falling on the slope, but I noticed that if we
> could get on to the rim itself we should not be underneath the
> main part of the shower of rocks.
>
> One boy had started running down the slope with all speed.
> I yelled to the second boy to stand still, and managed to stop
> him in time. We both moved up on to the rim itself. Hardly
> any rocks fell there, and the few that did we watched from
> underneath and ran away before they came down. It was a
> most weird experience. Huge masses were bounding down the
> slope with tremendous leaps, higher and higher, until they
> reached the bottom. They seemed to pursue the fleeing boy,
> who had already vanished in the dusky shadows. . . .[1]

Similar vivid descriptions with suitable vocabulary are available from old chronicles as well as from modern writers and
travellers such as W. H. Hudson, H. M. Tomlinson, and Peter

[1] *Camping Adventures in New Guinea*, by Evelyn Cheeseman
(Harrap, 1948), p. 132.

Fleming.[1] Such extracts are valuable also as starting-points for directed discussion.

All oral lessons should allow some time for individual work by the pupils. Generally this takes place during the latter half of the lesson but occasionally, with profit, the order might be reversed. Using textbooks, atlases, reference-books, and previous lesson notes, the pupils might be asked to offer solutions of simple, geographical problems such as, "Suggest reasons for the dense population of Java," or "Name the large towns on two alternative railway routes from London to Sheffield, and note any differences in the country they cross." The second half of the lesson would be devoted to consideration of some of the answers, and would be used to emphasize the important points and to remedy any serious omissions.

[1] A useful bibliography appears in *Handbook for Geography Teachers* (Methuen, 1960).

# I I

## Capes and Bays

IT is a commonplace to make fun of old-fashioned geography teaching in terms of learning the capes and bays, and indeed the parrot-fashion learning of earlier generations had nothing to recommend it. It is worthwhile considering, however, whether we may not have moved a little too far away from the learning of good honest facts : for all the attention we have given to teaching method we are not in agreement with those so-called progressive educationalists who maintain that it doesn't matter what is learnt so long as the manner of learning it is right.

We have stressed already the importance of using the geography time in the study of significant factual material and we have suggested that there is an inner core of factual knowledge in geography which is worth learning to be remembered. There is little doubt that the criticisms levelled against the teachers of geography from time to time by employers and others, that the young people recently left school do not know where places are, is by no means groundless. We would suggest that within this core of factual knowledge worth learning there is a place for learning where places are.

It may be worthwhile to consider two important aspects if this premise is to be accepted. First, what places? And, secondly, how should they be learnt? It is convenient to consider the method of learning first since the answer to the first of these two questions links up with other considerations as to the whole field of factual knowledge worth learning.

The modern counterpart of "capes and bays" is to expect our pupils at least to know the whereabouts on a map of the more important place-names. The vital difference is not that we should no longer learn where places are but that we should learn them visually and not verbally, certainly not parrot-fashion. Children's power to remember visually varies greatly just as their power to remember facts expressed verbally varies greatly : just as we cannot assume that when something has been read it is remembered, so we cannot assume that when something has been looked at on a map or in a picture it is remembered. If in the sphere of verbal knowledge we want a fact of history, a verse of poetry, or the meaning of a foreign word to be remembered then we have to take steps to see that it is learnt. Equally in geography, if we want the name of a river or an ocean or a place in a particular position to be remembered we have to see that it is learnt. The process, however, may be a different one since place-name knowledge is of a visual kind. The association of ideas which assists re-collection needs therefore to be a visual association. It is a properly geographical method as well as one which assists the learning process to mark a feature on a map and note its relationship with another feature : a town with a gap or a coalfield with an upland, for example. Moreover, whereas in the case of verbal knowledge an oral or written answer will suffice to test the learning, in the case of place-name know-ledge a visual means of testing the learning is required. The visual learning itself is in practice done best by oral question and answer in relation to a map of some kind, and, just as in the learning of arithmetical tables or spelling short spells of learning and testing at as frequent intervals as possible are best, so in place-name learning short but frequent spells of a similar kind will prove most successful. In practice, however, the teacher is faced with the sheer problem of arranging this since the test requires the map and the map is not always there. Individual ingenuity, of course, finds ways of over-coming this: last week's test-map may still, by careful con-triving, be on the back of the blackboard. Other teachers use outline-maps sometimes in white on black paper on which chalk can be used, which are prepared by a number of firms. Some teachers build up their own store of test sketch-maps with places and geographical features already marked upon them. There are also a few textbooks and notebooks published which give test-maps or, still better, problem-maps, which are useful for this purpose.

In our experience a most useful single permanent aid in this matter of place-name learning is a blackboard on which an outline-map of the world has been painted in white. If it is readily available frequent recourse to its use will enable quick reminders to be given of the whereabouts not only of the part of the world being dealt with in the lesson but of its relation-ship to other parts of the world, particularly, for example, to its position in relation to the home country and the lands or seas which would be passed over in reaching it. Certainly some devices are needed to make sure that a few basic outline-maps which can be used to help pupils learn the whereabouts of places are available.

It will be clear from what has been said that we are of the opinion that learning where places are is an essential though minor part of the geography course, and one in which direct teaching has a most important part to play. Let us not over-look, however, the kind of ancillary aids in this sphere available through the working of groups as described in an earlier chapter.

When we come to consider what place-names should be learned we enter, of course, a field where the discretion of the individual teacher is over-riding. There is little doubt that most geography teachers asked to give the place-names which they would expect to teach when dealing with a particular country would give lists in which there were a great many names in common. The fact that this result would have come about partly through the influence of textbooks and examination papers does not mean that the names which are common to all the lists are the wrong ones but probably, on the other hand, that they are the essential ones. Let us, however, consider two points which the teacher ought to have in mind in expecting place-names to be learnt. First, it is better for all the children in a class to learn properly all or nearly all the place-names put before them. An irregular result might come from too long a list and some pupils might never learn some of the most essential. In other words, the length of the list should vary with the ability of the class. In a knowledge of the where-abouts of places the distinction between the minimum core of factual knowledge and the larger surrounding area of signifi-cant and worth while but not essential knowledge is applicable, just as it is to other factual aspects of geography. A second point which we stress is that boys and girls should not be expected to *learn* the whereabouts of a place until the reason for wanting to know where it is has become clear. To put it another way, we want to know where a place is and learn something about its significance at the same time. It is, there-fore, in our view, a grave mistake to introduce the study of a new country or continent by providing an outline-map asking for a dozen or so place-names to be marked on it and then expecting those place-names to be learnt. They are at present meaningless and without reality. The whereabouts of places and rivers and mountains and so forth should be introduced when those places or features are met or described. The real learning of their whereabouts should come when there is some hope that interest in the reality of the feature will have been aroused and some knowledge about the place or the feature will be recalled.

We have devoted a good deal of attention to the learning of place-names since this area of geographical information is one of practical advantage. In the bread-and-butter sense there are many jobs in which it is useful to know where important places are : in a more general sense an educated person needs a minimum at least of this kind of knowledge as the background to his daily life, to his reading of the paper, to his approach to public affairs, to his intelligent conversation with his neighbours. It is probably true that for children of average ability the visual memory is better than the verbal memory, and a good training in the learning of significant place-names by visual and not verbal means may very well have a lasting effect.

When we come to consider other kinds of factual geographical information which ought really to be learnt, again we would probably find that the individual discretion of teachers in this matter would give results somewhat similar in each case. We attempt to consider this in more detail in the next chapter but stress now that the amount of sheer information which we ought to expect pupils to learn must necessarily vary according to the ability of the pupils, and that the facts themselves must be significant. The same principle of learning after interest has been aroused and description given which we suggested in respect of place-names applies to facts of physical and economic geography. The direct teaching and learning must always be in small doses. It must always be lively and interesting, and it must always have a visual relationship. To learn the products of a place without knowing where the place is, is to do less than half the job and suggests an unreality of approach. It is regrettably the case that those who act as examiners for public examinations too often find that candidates supply a good deal of factual information, and then, inadvertently, give themselves away by showing that they do not know whereabouts on a map these economic or human or physical facts belong. Any factual information learnt must first be descriptively realistic and, second, must be properly located.

Perhaps we may be permitted a final word about distance.

It is a commonplace to remark upon the shrinking of distances in the modern world, and we would expect to get across to our pupils significant ideas about the world relationship of peoples and places. It is worthwhile trying to give them a reasonable idea of the sheer distances involved. We do not suggest, of course, the learning of mileage or hours' flying time, but we do suggest that all boys and girls should leave school with some realistic idea of the *order* of distance of different parts of their own country, of other countries, and other continents from their homeland. It is sad, for example, to find in a class of fourteen-year-olds the inability to answer whether it is 300 or 3000 or 30,000 miles across the Atlantic, and some tests given not long since to students entering training colleges—all of them presumably with Ordinary Level passes in the G.C.E. but not necessarily in geography—showed that even these future teachers could be several hundred per cent. out in their estimation of distances from their home country to some parts of the world.

The use of the world map mentioned earlier gives an opportunity for frequent brief reference to world distances. The general principle of approaching regional study from the large-scale to the smaller equally provides the opportunity to draw attention to distance. We would think, in short, that part of the core of minimum geographical information worth learning is some reasonable idea of the length and breadth of the land, and some modest approximation to not wholly erroneous information about distances on a world scale.

# 12

## What Shall We Teach?

THE "bi-polar" aspect of education which invokes the interaction of pupils and teacher is matched by another dualism—that of pupil and subject-matter. The teacher is not only concerned in teaching geography but in teaching John Smith geography. No teaching is successful unless it is fully aware of the pupil as an individual, paying attention to his rate of working, his special interests, his mental capacity, his emotional response, his attitude to the community of which he is a part, as well as to his misdemeanours and his shortcomings.

All good teachers realize this, but they are also well aware that the pupil has to be taught a certain body of knowledge, valuable because it is significant, which is only one stage in the educational process. Perhaps more important must be the training in the *use* of facts and practice in applying them in new situations and in making deductions from them. In other words the pupil has to be taught how to think—a very difficult task indeed.

In preparation for this the pupil has to acquire significant factual information, valuable for its own sake, about which to think. This is a fundamental requirement in any subject or activity, and its acquirement may be an important factor in the development of character. As A. N. Whitehead says, "The only avenue towards knowledge is by discipline in the acquirement of ordered fact."[1] The rate of acquisition and the quantity will depend on the mental calibre of the pupil, but in geography, as in other subjects, a body of basic knowledge is essential. The need for this basic knowledge in most subjects is taken for granted; nobody disputes the necessity of knowing the multiplication table in arithmetic, certain basic rules in English, irregular verbs in French, the staff notation in music, and, at a higher level, the periodic table in chemistry. Similarly no geography teacher should be shy of maintaining that *part* of his work is to ensure that his pupils learn a certain amount of fundamental geographical knowledge. There was a phase in the teaching of the subject not so many years ago when more emphasis was placed on the ability to draw inferences and apply principles than in the learning of accurate fact, but a more balanced attitude is prevalent to-day.

As we have stressed, ability to make deductions and to think logically is the essence of real education but it cannot be exercised in a vacuum; some facts have got to be known. As was stressed in the last chapter, the body of factual knowledge which the less able pupil can acquire, understand, and apply is less than that of his more gifted academic fellow. The selection of the most suitable material for any pupil is a difficult task because the primary knowledge required in geography is not well defined as it is in arithmetic or English or French. The superficial answer to the question which heads this chapter might be, "Begin at the beginning and go as far and as fast as the ability of the pupils will permit," but the experienced geography teacher knows that this simple answer is unhelpful. For young children learning to read there is an obvious beginning, whichever method, phonic or visual, is adopted. In the early stages of number-teaching there are well-defined and essential first steps, and even with more advanced mathematical ideas the experts would probably agree on the

[1] *The Aims of Education*, by A. N. Whitehead (Williams and Norgate, 1932), p. 47.

essential fundamental stages in algebra or geometry. In physics and chemistry there are obvious first principles, easily taught and capable of practical demonstration, which can form the introductory work.

The situation is different in geography. The same question, similarly worded, could be set for the General Certificate at Ordinary Level and for an Honours degree, but each would result in answers of very different quality. The problem is not only one of beginning but of content. Most teachers now agree that the geography of the locality provides the logical, educational starting-point, but there remains the problem of what to include in the local study, and what to do or omit after that. The whole world provides the subject-matter, and what to include and what to leave out provides a very difficult problem. Careful selection from the wide range of suitable material is essential so that the limited time available may be used to the best advantage. Agreement among teachers as to what constitutes the essential minimum which ought to be covered by any secondary-school course would probably be unobtainable, nor, indeed, is complete uniformity desirable, but the problem may be clarified if we attempt in broad terms to indicate the desirable scope of the course.

Local geography, as discussed in previous chapters, must be included for several reasons. It stresses the reality of the subject-matter because the local environment is real to the pupil. It provides a necessary means of comparison of the unknown to the known whether it be in the quantity of rainfall, the height of a mountain, the size of a town, or the nature of agricultural activity. It allows the demonstration of one of the basic aims of geographical study—namely, the comparisons of distributions and the emphasis on relationships. It encourages habits of observation, and it may lay the foundations of civic interest and pride. The scope of the locality study will depend on the nature of the district, whether it is urban or rural, on the inclination of the teacher, and, to some extent, on the attitude of the head teacher. The aim should be to keep a balance between the physical geography and human activity, to bring out relationships, to encourage observation, and to show how to record the results. In the process, by means already developed in Chapter 7, Ordnance Survey maps will be read and understood through being constantly in use.

The emphasis in the syllabus as a whole may fall on the human aspects of the subject, especially with the slower and younger pupils; but we must never lose sight of the simpler aspects of physical geography, which form the bases of the subject. We have in mind the work of rivers, the way of the weather, the action of ice in modifying the landscape, for example, as well as consideration of the major terrestrial phenomena such as the explanation of day and night and the seasons. Thirdly, regional studies of certain parts of the world are essential, and lastly the course should aim to give attention to systematic geography, which can allow consideration of the earth as a whole, and the intimate relationship of all its parts in the rapid developments of to-day.

Many teachers prefer to include the physical geography as part of the local and regional sections of the syllabus. The work of rivers in erosion, transportation, and deposition, for example, may be considered when the regional study deals with the Mississippi or the Hwang Ho basin, the nature and formation of fiords when Norway is the subject, the action of moving ice when the Alps are described, and so on. This can work well providing there has been careful planning beforehand to ensure inclusion of the most important aspects. These are not difficult to select since any simple textbook in physical geography will show the essential items.

The greatest problem is to decide as to the content of the regional part of the syllabus, for all parts of the world *might* be included but, in practice, some must be omitted. Are there any principles which may be applied to help in narrowing the field of choice?

Some parts of the world are more important to British pupils than to others because they are linked culturally or politically with this country. Thus the larger members of the British Commonwealth of Nations and the most significant parts of the United States are more important than Indonesia, Madagascar, or Manchuria. Nearness is a guide. The countries of western Continental Europe are more important to pupils here than Turkey or Rumania. Then some parts of the world may be introduced because they demonstrate well some geographical principles. Andean Bolivia, for example, might be included because it brings out the difficulties of living and working in high altitudes; details of agriculture in Sicily might serve to illustrate human eagerness to utilize volcanic soil in spite of danger and difficulty; on other grounds these two areas might be omitted. Regions might be brought into the syllabus in order that certain current events might be placed in their geographical settings, on other occasions they would probably not appear. There might not be time, normally, for consideration of the Pacific Islands, but news of a serious volcanic eruption in one of them might provide the opportunity for topical reference, not only to volcanoes in general but to the more detailed geography of the particular island.

The other large section—the General or Systematic—needs careful handling because it can lead to vagueness and generalization. The aim should be that by the end of the course the world pattern of vegetation or climatic regions should become apparent. This means that reference to world regions will be linked with the more specific regional work, an approach which will probably be more successful than that which takes each type of climate or vegetation in turn until they have all been considered.

Even when these methods of reducing the content of the syllabus have been applied, probably still too much remains for satisfactory attention, especially with the slower classes. The solution is to apply some form of "sampling." In this method, for example, considerable attention with reasonable detail might be given to the conditions under which the natives of the Amazon forest live, in order to illustrate life in the equatorial forests of the world, and less time would be devoted to the Congo Basin or the Malayan forest. On the other hand, work on a tropical plantation might be illustrated by rubber cultivation in Malaya, and in this case Ceylon's rubber industry would receive only passing mention, not because it is unimportant but because the interest-provoking detail has been provided in the Malayan lessons and serves to illustrate the technique employed in Ceylon.

Sampling is also possible when the approach is by topics. When the topic is "Wool," and sheep-rearing is under consideration, then details of work on a New South Wales sheep-station will receive more attention than, say, the Patagonian *estancia*; in the manufacturing aspect probably the West Riding will take precedence over New England. If the topic is "Mountains" the nature of ranges, the work of the people, and the difficulties of transport in, say, a part of the Rockies, will serve to exemplify conditions in other Alpine fold-mountain areas, and the East African plateau, those of other plateau lands.

The general practitioner may feel some hesitation in attempting to compile a syllabus which involves sampling for fear that important regions or aspects are omitted, or he may be uncertain as to the relative significance he ought to give to various portions of the subject-matter. Some help may be derived from the study of reputable textbooks designed for the particular age group being taught. Comparison between several different examples will provide some consensus of opinion; it will indicate what other experts have thought significant.

In 1950-51 the School Broadcasting Council undertook an inquiry in schools in connexion with their geographical broadcasts as they were related to school syllabuses. As a result of a large number of replies from secondary schools the Council were able to say, "At the Secondary stage syllabuses were usually expressed in terms of countries or continents, and most seemed to be designed to cover the main regions of the world in a four- (or sometimes three-) year course."[1] The general pattern of the first three years was similar—the British Isles received the most attention, the remainder of Europe and the other Continents were touched on—but there was more variation in the fourth year when aspects of the world as a whole were included.

No doubt a national census would show that a regional syllabus based on countries and continents is the most common form, but there is a growing feeling that the topic approach, or variations on this, is more suited to the slower, less academically minded pupil. A scheme combining topics and regions which has proved successful is fully dealt with in the next chapter.

Meanwhile it may be helpful to add a note on some of the various ways of putting together the agreed material of the geography course. Those who aim to meet the needs of an external examination will probably feel that a regional syllabus is essential and the question arises as to what is the best order of arrangement. In broad outline such a syllabus might read :

*First Year:* local geography and the British Isles (with emphasis on the occupations of the people)
*Second Year:* the Southern Continents
*Third Year:* North America and Asia
*Fourth Year:* Europe outside the British Isles
*Fifth Year:* British Isles (regionally) and General World Geography

Ordnance Survey map work would be introduced through field excursions and in connexion with Local Study, physical and mathematical geography incidentally when they were most relevant. Thus the subject of "Time" might arise in con-

[1] *Geography and School Broadcasting,* The School Broadcasting Council (N.D.).

nexion with cricket in Australia in the Second Year or in connexion with Time Zones on a journey across the United States; the significance of soil types in influencing variations in agriculture might find a place in the Fourth Year when France is under discussion. Some teachers might prefer to have the Americas in the Second Year and Monsoon Asia, Africa, and Australia in the next. One advantage of this arrangement is that the whole range of climatic regions is introduced in the Second Year; on the other hand many feel that the Southern Continents are easier for pupils in their Second Year because there is comparatively little industrialization. Others would introduce the British Commonwealth of Nations in one of these years, arguing, *inter alia*, that a wide range of climatic types would be included. If a similar scheme is needed for a Four-Year Course then some parts of each region would have to be omitted after careful consideration of their relative significance. Such a scheme might be :

*First Year:* local geography, the British Isles (with emphasis on the chief occupations of the people), aspects of North America

*Second Year:* the Southern Continents and parts of Monsoon Asia

*Third Year:* parts of Continental Europe and some of the remainder of Asia

*Fourth Year:* the British Isles in its World Setting and General Geography

Some have argued that the Regional Syllabus is not suited to the non-academic type of pupil, and certain disadvantages are touched upon in the next chapter. A possible alternative is the syllabus based entirely on topics of which "Foodstuffs, Sources of Power, Minerals, Irrigation, Trade Routes, Forests" might be examples. Each aspect would be considered in its world setting, but care has to be taken that the geographical nature of the work is maintained, and special provision has to be made for Local Geography and Map Study.

A related scheme is the theme study in which each theme provides work for one year, thus :

*First Year:* Food, Shelter, Clothing (in selected representative parts of the world)

*Second Year:* Getting about (the use of maps, means of transport, the influence of relief on routes, etc., in different parts of the world)

*Third Year:* Climates and their Effects

*Fourth Year:* Industry and Trade. Living in a Community (emphasis on Local Geography and the British Isles)

These last two schemes have the advantage of providing opportunity for revision since any part of the world can be considered again from a different angle, and they are "concentric" in that successively the local region, the British Isles, and the rest of the world can provide illustrations for each topic or theme.

There is room for experiment and variety in forms of syllabus even when they must include the requirements of an external examination. A good syllabus must suit the quality and interests of the pupils who are going to study it and the teacher who is going to teach it. Whatever the scheme, it should be drawn up in considerable detail to show clearly the ground to be covered. The syllabus which says, "The British Isles by Regions," or "The Chief Trade Routes of the World," or "The Chief Commodities of Commerce," gives little guidance to the hard-pressed teacher who needs to know which regions of the British Isles and which routes and commodities are to be taken. Unimaginative and undesirable because it is open to abuse is the syllabus which merely transcribes the chapter-headings of the pupils' classbook. The syllabus which receives careful thought, and takes into account all the relevant factors, and sets out the result fully, is a great help to the teacher both in giving direction to the work and in ensuring that the necessary preparatory thinking has been undertaken well before the course is given.

# 13

## The Concentric Syllabus

WE are very much aware that the selection of the material to be included in the geography syllabus is a matter for the individual teacher and that the whole pattern and framework of the syllabus are a matter for the individual school. Whatever individual variations there may be in the choice of material, there are important educational issues involved in the decision on the kind of syllabus which is to be arranged. It may, for example, affect the whole learning of geography in a school quite radically if one pattern of syllabus is chosen in preference to another. Certainly some kinds of work which we have described and the approach to the work which has been suggested in earlier chapters are easier to accomplish if the syllabus follows a broadly concentric pattern rather than any other.

We should not wish to appear to suggest that there is anything fundamentally wrong about a geography syllabus formed on another pattern, but in our view there are disadvantages in other ways of arranging the material of the geography course, and advantages in a concentric arrangement of it which make us wish at least to urge upon teachers the desirability of considering the kind of pattern we propose, always, of course, adapting it to their own particular needs and interests, and embodying within it the particular content which they hold to be the most important.

We have already used a phrase—"the concentric syllabus"

—which may not convey a clear meaning to all who read it, and it will be best, therefore, first to give a simple definition.

This kind of syllabus is one in which the basic plan of work covering a period of, say, several weeks is that in which attention is first given to the local or at least near-at-hand, then to a home country or European area, and then to an example or a region chosen from a more distant part of the world. It is important to add the association with this series of basically regional studies of an aspect of general geography and to envisage the proper use of maps, including large-scale maps, in the kinds of ways suggested in an earlier chapter. The thread running through this concentric pattern of regional studies will be a theme or topic linking them together and associating them with the aspect of general geography referred to.

Having defined our purpose, let us now, before elaborating its working out, give some further indication of why we hold this to be a valuable approach. Most teachers of geography become aware of the danger of regional work becoming disconnected, and of studies in general geography, particularly physical geography, becoming insufficiently related to regional work. There is, in addition, the danger referred to earlier of detaching the study of large-scale maps as a separate item within the course. In any good geography syllabus there are these two basic parts: regional studies of at any rate the more important areas in the world and general studies on a world basis of important aspects of geography, whether physical or human. We ought not to exclude either of these. In our view regional study is fundamental to the character of the whole subject, for it is in the descriptive analysis of all the varied geographical aspects of an area, in the recognition of inter-relationships between different aspects, and in the attempt to make a synthesis of the whole, and epitomize the geography of the area in a kind of personality sketch, that the geographer carries out his most fundamental task. Without the attempt to see a region whole, true geographical understanding cannot be developed, and the inevitable tendencies, in a subject whose main task is to correlate, towards moving away from the core of the subject out into the other fields of knowledge dealt with by other specialisms, lead to the disintegration of the subject itself. On the other hand, the regional approach cannot be made with proper understanding unless patterns on a world scale, both physical and human, and general principles in the broad field of physical geography are properly understood. As we have already remarked in the preceding chapter, boys and girls must be given, for example, some understanding of the weather, or of the work of rivers, and ought to be introduced to some ideas on a world scale of such things as the pattern of climates, the pattern of population distribution in the world as a whole, the main outlines of international trade, and of routes by land, sea, and air.

If our syllabus is basically regional it is possible, but not easy, to integrate the general geography with it. It is simpler, but less educational, to interrupt regional studies by periods of the study of general geography. But this is not really satisfactory, and the sense of reality which is so essential is most likely to be achieved, particularly in the field of physical geography, if what is taught in that field is clearly seen to have meaning in terms of particular parts of the earth's surface. It is possible, of course, to do this in relation to a syllabus where basically the world is studied continent by continent.

This brings us, therefore, to a further factor which we feel suggests preference for a concentric rather than a continent-by-continent pattern of regional work. It is that in studying one particular continent, say, for a whole term, the sense of relationship to other parts of the world, and particularly to the home country, tends to be lost, and the sense of scale compared with regions of the homeland or with what is known in the regional sense at first-hand is difficult, if not to establish, at least to maintain. There are further difficulties. Under a continent-by-continent pattern some parts of the world will be visited and learnt about once and for all, except perhaps for a hurried return in a term or so of high-pressure revision in the fifth year. Thus lands studied early in the secondary course may have faded badly from the minds of the boys and girls by the end of the course. If, on the other hand, within each period of work some regional study is undertaken in the homeland and in distant lands, or, better still, in the homeland, in Europe, and in another continent, there is the necessity from time to time to return to each continent, and, in relation to the new region being studied, to pick up the threads of earlier studies in the same continent. Such ideas as relationship on a world scale in terms of routes and trade fall naturally into place, and size and distance, which we have suggested earlier deserve some attention, may be dealt with in a way which is clearly purposeful. If the regions are linked together by a suitable theme that will in itself generally be an opportunity to bring within the period of work concerned some aspect of general geography which again will have purpose and meaning because of this relationship. Moreover, different themes, while calling for successive additions to the field of general geography covered, will equally give opportunities for revision of, and building upon, aspects of general geography which have been met at earlier stages.

The suggestion that the concentric pattern may begin locally has its own value and will almost certainly appeal to geography teachers, most of whom now recognize the importance of local study. While fully accepting this importance, we have some reservations about long stretches of detailed local study. If some aspect of the locality can, without artificiality, be associated with the theme which links the regional studies, then there is seen to be validity in this particular piece of local study, and there is the additional advantage that it can be properly integrated with studies of other parts of the home country and of the world. Such local study will call for the use of large-scale maps and will be a further contribution towards the plan outlined in an earlier chapter for learning about maps by using them rather than by having lessons on them in isolation.

A concentric syllabus, when it has been finally drawn up, will appear as a series of themes or topics, perhaps three or four in each term, within each of which there will be a few regions to be studied, perhaps some local study together with some aspect of general geography. The sum total of these topics, of course, has got to cover the regional content which we regard as essential for the whole syllabus together with the physical and human geography in the general sense that we think essential. It may well be that this pattern is best employed for a four-year course and that where a fifth year is taken that year might be devoted to revision on a continent basis.

It will be clear that within the items of study proposed for any particular theme, there will the opportunity for choice. We have stressed already that the geography course will cover a minimum area of factual knowledge to be learnt and a much larger area of factual knowledge, not all of it necessarily to be learnt. We would suggest, therefore, that within each theme there would be items which all forms would be expected to study because of their importance, though not necessarily in the same degree of detail, together with other items which would be optional in two senses : first, in the sense that more of them would be taken by the more able forms and more omitted by the less able, and, secondly, that among them the individual preference of the teacher or the choice of the form itself would operate so that the regions chosen were the ones which commanded the most interest.

At this point it may be wise to show how such a syllabus might be constructed. We would feel that the first step is to draw up lists of regions under the headings of "The British Isles," "Europe," "The Rest of the World," which are felt to be sufficiently significant to merit inclusion, and then to mark in each of those three lists the regions that are essential for all pupils. In passing, let us admit that we are quite frankly accepting the fact that there are some parts of the world of which regional studies cannot be made within the time available for geography in most secondary schools. The next step would be similarly to list the aspects of general geography which ought to receive attention, and similarly to divide them between essential and optional. The third step is to provide oneself with a list of possible themes or topics. It is important not to regard these themes as the dominating factors in the syllabus; they are merely the vehicles for carrying the items which we wish to include. We need, therefore, a long list of possible themes, some of which may not in the end be needed. Some will be products—wheat, fruit, cattle, iron, and steel; others may be physical—mountains, islands, volcanoes; others may be human—canals, trans-continental railways, water transport. When these lists have been drawn up the next step is to allocate regions from the different lists and items of general geography to appropriate themes, balancing the allocation to any particular theme in such a way that the pattern of work called for in following it is along the concentric lines proposed. When a theme has been arranged in this way it is possible to add, in some but not all cases, suitable items of local geography.

The group of work now associated with each theme has now to be placed at an appropriate point in the course as a whole. To a considerable extent it will be found that some of the themes are associated with aspects of general geography that need to be dealt with earlier, and carry regional studies on the whole of simpler areas, while some other themes involve aspects of general geography which need to be taken later, and are associated with more complex regions. For example, "Wheat" carries the idea of simple climatic limits, and links up with temperate grasslands. On the other hand "Iron and Steel" suggests general ideas of ore distribution and metal content, and rather less simple relationships of an economic kind. Up to a point the study of general geography involves a degree of progression which means that the order in which the aspects are studied is important, and, in so far as particular aspects of general geography are necessarily associated with particular themes, this consideration is likely to be a determining factor in placing the themes in order in the course as a whole. Nevertheless, the varied aspects of general geography do not form a single progressive series, and there is considerable latitude in the arrangement of the themes even when this factor is taken into account. There is little doubt that some regional studies are much more suitable for younger pupils and others for older pupils, and it is likely that when the themes have provisionally been arranged in order some re-allocation of individual regions to different themes from those originally chosen will be seen to be desirable. This is by no means impossible for, particularly in the case of the more complex regions, one of several important aspects may be the one used to form the link between the particular regional study and the group of work as a whole. One or two examples may help to make this clear. Among the themes which would suggest themselves for early study in the course would be the ones associated with major primary products, particularly major items of food or some simple physical themes such as mountains or deserts. In very many cases the regions of Britain, of Europe, and of other parts of the world, which come to mind as being linked together by one of these simple themes, are in themselves relatively simple regions—East Anglia and the Prairies, in connexion with wheat, for example, or the Lake District and British Columbia with the study of mountains. The Mediterranean region of Europe as a wheat-producing area or Switzerland as a mountainous country, on the other hand, would not be appropriately associated, say, with first-year work on the themes of wheat and mountains respectively, the former because probably some building up of understanding of climates would be needed before the region can be properly approached, and the latter because the total regional geography of Switzerland, if the country is to be taken as a whole and not simply its Alpine area studied, is quite complex and more appropriate to third- or fourth-year work. At the other end of the scale themes such as textiles or iron and steel are probably more appropriate to older boys and girls, involving some understanding of basic ideas of economic geography, and calling for the study of quite complex industrial areas. The North-east Coast region of Britain, Lancastria, the Westphalian industrial area, the middle Appalachian-Great-Lakes region of North America, are all of them areas which are probably better studied later in the course rather than earlier.

Although what has been said may make the form of syllabus proposed appear complicated, as indeed it is, it is in another sense an illustration of its flexibility, for the careful adjustment of the arrangement of regions in relation to the themes, and to the stage in the course at which each theme is taken, make it possible to arrive at a very careful grading of the difficulty of the various individual items of the syllabus. A continent-by-continent syllabus, on the other hand, necessarily calls for the study within a particular term of some areas whose geography is relatively simple, and with which relatively simple aspects of general geography are appropriately associated, and also, in the case at any rate of most continents, of other regions much more complex in their geography, and involving considerations of general geography, whether on the physical or human side, that are appropriate to the later stages of the course. The home country itself is the most striking example of this difficulty. Europe, because it contains so many difficult regions, is usually studied late in the course under a continent-by-continent syllabus but nevertheless includes some more simple regions that are appropriately studied earlier, and some countries, such as those of Southern

Europe, which, within the context of a secondary-school course and at the level of detail appropriate to pupils of average ability, are readily included in the second- or third-year rather than later. North America is another striking example of a continent comprised of regions some of which are relatively simple and others quite complex.

We do not propose to set out a detailed example of a syllabus constructed on the concentric method although one has been included elsewhere.[1] It is in the opportunity for individual choice and in the detailed adjustment of the many individual items in the syllabus, which is possible under this proposed pattern, that much of its value lies, and it would be quite wrong if any teacher who wished to use a syllabus on these lines were to do other than construct his own. Even when he has done this the syllabus which he has arrived at will undoubtedly be subject to further modification and adjustment, and it is hoped that it will always carry within it the opportunity for variation, not only from year to year but as between one teacher and his colleagues, and as between the work of one form and that of another with the same teacher, in the light of the particular interests of each form.

Where a school is large enough to have within it courses of varying length, and where these courses in their later stages include within them special studies looking towards subsequent employment, such as studies in commerce or engineering, the pattern of syllabus here proposed makes it very possible for the work of a particular class to be oriented towards their special study without the whole framework of the syllabus being changed.

In a large school there is an obvious advantage in the general pattern of the syllabus being common to all classes, but it is equally desirable that the geography studied by those whose special study is engineering should have a somewhat

[1] See *Geography in the Secondary School* (Geographical Association, 1960).

different slant from that studied by those whose special study is commerce or some other field. The flexibility of the concentric syllabus and the opportunities for choice which have been mentioned make this possible perhaps to a greater degree than with the traditional type of syllabus which, because of its relative inflexibility, is often replaced in schools where special studies with a vocational bias have been established by syllabuses of a totally different kind. The danger of a geography syllabus geared closely to special studies of this kind is that it may become unbalanced from a geographical point of view and, in seeking to establish good links with the special interest of the pupils, may fail to be true geography. In practical terms this often means that the geography syllabus may become a syllabus in economic geography or industrial geography, and that the regional studies, which we regard as the core of the subject, making possible as they do the recognition of geographical interrelationships and calling for the attempt to epitomize the whole geographical personality of an area of the earth's surface, will be omitted.

A good syllabus in any subject is very much a matter of balance and needs to be drawn up with a clear idea in mind of what is fundamental to the subject as an educational discipline and as a contribution towards the whole development of the boy or girl. Interest in subsequent employment is only part of this whole development, a part which ought to have its place in considering the syllabus of each subject but not one which ought to outweigh the over-riding conception of the subject as part of a liberal secondary education.

# 14

## Recording and Testing the Facts

HAVING decided what we shall teach, and having arranged our syllabus, we cannot afford to overlook the necessity to ensure that the selected facts are really known by the pupils and to find out if this is in fact the case. Consideration may be given to two slightly different requirements —the testing of facts recently taught and the testing of the work done over a longer period, say a term or a year. Several methods for achieving the former are well known. "Slip" tests involving answers of only a few words, the filling-in with suitable words of spaces in given sentences, the marking of features on outline-maps, are frequent and useful devices, but it may be that these rather academic and unimaginative forms of factual revision may be more suited to the brighter pupils. The others may find greater stimulation and interest in a simple activity which represents some form of challenge. Thus, rather than the pupil copying and "learning" a given sketch-map, it might be better if the map is set in puzzle form, after the fashion of Figure 13. Such a map can be used to teach facts for the first time by challenging the class to find the missing information from textbook or atlas, or it can be used to revise facts already taught, the pupils writing down the solution in a given time, in a test. Maps such as these can be easily duplicated and used many times since the answers need not be written on the maps. Sometimes the basic information—*e.g.*, of relief or coastline—may be copied by the

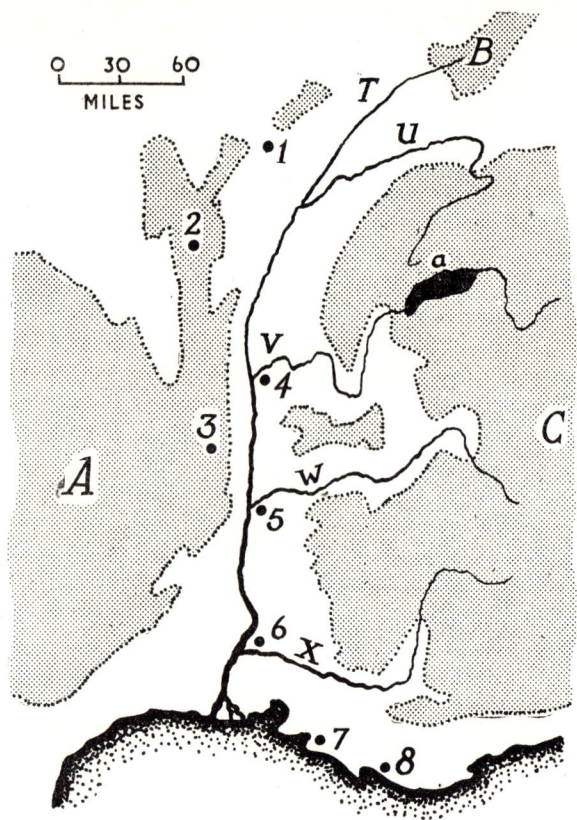

Fig. 13. A Test Map: the Rhône Valley

pupils into their notebooks, and new facts, such as the route of a main railway, the location of a coalfield, the position of an important airfield, learned in a lesson or culled from the reference source, may be added.

Reference has already been made to the testing of place-name knowledge in Chapter 11, but we may add that outline-maps for individual work and the marking of locational features should be used with discretion and restraint. Too frequent resort to this device unrelated to other forms of teaching and activity might be the equivalent of "capes and bays" geography returning in a different guise. Sometimes pupils are asked in an *introductory* lesson, say on Africa, to mark the five main rivers and six important ports. This is unsound because such material should be taught to the pupils in relation to other geographical information; pupils cannot be expected to know, merely by looking at an atlas, which are the chief rivers or the main ports. If the purpose is to stress the location of these features the better approach is to write the names on the blackboard and to ask the pupils to enter them on the maps with the aid of the atlas; but this is best done when the names have real significance for the pupils.

The so-called "memory assisted tests," in which pupils are invited to make a selection from given facts in order to answer questions, have been much used in America. The credit which could be derived from guessing is eliminated by subtracting the number of answers wrong from the number right if a numerical result is required. For example :

Which of the following numbers is nearest to the population of Greater London—2,000,000   8,000,000   15,000,000 550,000?

Which of the following commodities are likely to be important exports from San Francisco—coal, tinned peaches, cane sugar, dried fruit?

Select from the annual rainfall averages given below the most likely amounts for each of the following towns—Manchester, Oban, Cambridge, Newcastle, 56″ 35″ 68″ 28″ 23″

Which of the following crops are grown in Victoria, Australia—wheat, cane sugar, coffee, apples, millet?

In which of the following counties could you see (a) granite hills, (b) chalk hills—Sussex, Durham, Cornwall, Dorset, Cumberland?

Similar in type are the following :

Draw a line to represent the main railway route from London (Kings Cross) to Edinburgh, and mark along it the following stations in their correct order—York, Grantham, Newcastle, Berwick, Peterborough.

Repeat for the route from Calais to Milan, marking Dijon, Paris, Lyons, Turin.

The following lines represent the ranges of temperature at these towns—London, Moscow, Paris, Berlin.

|_____|

|_____|

|_____|

|_____|

Copy the lines and write below each the name of the appropriate town.

At intervals it will be desirable to carry out more comprehensive examinations to test work taught over a long period, say a term or a year. The pattern of these is well known, but a few comments may not be out of place. The setting of examination papers is an art which requires a great deal of thought and care. Apart from the obvious need to make wording perfectly clear yet concise, it is necessary to try to assess the probable reaction of the question on the pupil and to gauge the kind of answer it is likely to invoke. Careful consideration has to be given to the proper balance in the allocation of marks to various parts of the question, and this should be done first when it is set, not when the answer is being considered.

The essay type of answer may demand too much from the duller pupil. Questions should be short and simple, requiring brief sentences or paragraphs in answer, and as often as possible non-verbal forms should be required—additions to a given sketch-map or drawing a diagram or identifying mineral or vegetable specimens. Experiments might be tried with tests which require a variety of skills as well as practice in language and number. Thus in connexion with irrigation in Egypt the pupil might be invited to make a simple model of a shaduf, using the materials supplied, then to write a short paragraph saying why irrigation is needed, to make a simple diagram of a peasant-holding where the shaduf might be situated, and to mark the possible crops in the fields, and perhaps to calculate the weight of water lifted in a normal day's working, given the capacity of the bucket.

Pictures have an important part to play in the teaching of geography and they can be a stimulating and effective means of testing knowledge gained and the ability to think and make deductions. The naming or describing of portrayed physical features or human activities, the recognition of typical scenes from given regions or countries, the making of inferences about climate from the evidence in the picture, are but a few of the obvious possibilities. In addition, pictures used with discretion may help to enlarge, clarify, and make more accurate the pupil's geographical vocabulary. The shortage of suitable pictures may be overcome by the projection of selected frames from a film strip, which can be used for written tests since only a partial blackout is required. In fact, a variation of the "slip" test is possible for the teacher can pose the short oral question relevant to the feature in the picture which he points to while the pupils write the brief answer. Well-known and useful tests may be set on pictures of landscapes in conjunction with Ordnance Survey maps of the same area. Low, oblique aerial photographs might be used more for depicting physical or cultural surface features. Some have been successful with the making of diagrammatic sketches by pupils from pictures, for example, of an English farm or an Argentinian *estancia*.

A few words may not be out of place with regard to the pupil's notebook and the part it can play in good geography-teaching. The notebook may be used for writing exercises or working examples: it may be filled with work which is a model of its kind and calculated to impress the visiting inspector, it may serve as a record of the course and provide material for revision, or it may combine a number of these functions.

The younger pupils of secondary schools are generally incapable of real, effective revision from their own notes; even older children are often unable to master the considerable effort of concentration required, and they need to be taught how to revise properly. The notebook which is a perfect example of accuracy and neatness takes a great deal of time but there is something to be said for the attempt at perfection which it exemplifies. Occasionally such efforts are worthwhile, especially if they are intended for very special purposes, but only if they are infrequent; otherwise the work can become stultifying, uneducational, and time-consuming, and of little value in the geographical progress of the pupil. Some will remember the superlative examples of cartography produced by some pupils forty or fifty years ago during the lesson called "Mapping," which added little to their comprehension of geography.

It is understandable that a teacher should regard the note-book as a form of record which will indicate the main points of the work attempted, but it is undesirable that work in the notebook should be the only form in which the pupil expresses himself, and dictated or copied notes generally occupy time which could be used more profitably in other ways. A little consideration on the part of the teacher will ensure that the notebook provides a record of the work done and also a place in which the pupil attempts useful, thoughtful work. Pertinent written matter may be secured by asking for short answers to very specific questions which have been chosen to emphasize the points the pupil should know as a result of the lesson : the "reproduction knowledge" already referred to. The answers may require a few sentences or the names of places or substances or the drawing of a diagram or simple map. For example, after a lesson on agriculture on the Argentinian pampas the questions might be :

(1) Give three reasons why the pampas are suitable for the cultivation of wheat.
(2) Name three important crops of the pampas other than wheat.
(3) Write a few short sentences to describe the tenant-farmer's house.
(4) Make a drawing of (a) a wind pump, (b) a maize cob.

The nature of the questions would be adjusted to the intellectual calibre of the pupils. Those who found the mechanics of written English a major obstacle might have fewer literal answers (but not complete omission), and more drawing or collecting, with the addition, perhaps, of individual oral questions.

In the course of the lesson the teacher may have built up a sketch-map on the blackboard, and it is understandable that he should want his pupils to have a copy in their notebooks as part of the record, and to give them practice in the important art of sketch-map drawing. But mere copying from the board is an unstimulating, mechanical task requiring little mental effort. The pupil can be encouraged to think about what he is doing if he is asked to cull additional data from textbook or atlas, and enter it on the map. Or some of the information on the blackboard-map—e.g., the key or the name of a town—might be erased and the notebook map completed from memory. Figure 14 gives a simple example. The notebook used in this way will benefit the pupil and at the same time demonstrate to the teacher the effectiveness of his teaching, and, perhaps, the need for further explanation when general misunderstandings occur. Needless to say, careful attention to what the pupils set down will be part of the conscientious teacher's concern.

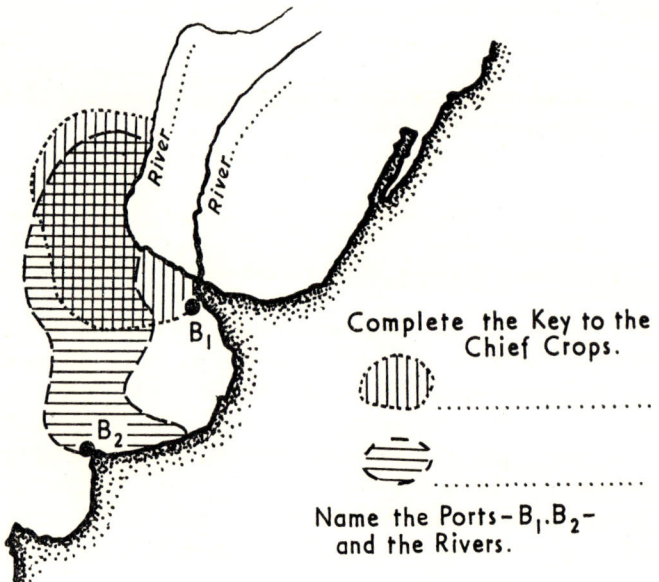

Complete the Key to the Chief Crops.

Name the Ports—B₁.B₂— and the Rivers.

Fig. 14. A MAP FOR THE NOTEBOOK: AGRICULTURE IN ARGENTINA

Testing and recording are only parts, and probably minor parts, of the many aspects of the teacher's work. Interest and mental stimulation will most likely arise when the pupil is exploring new fields in the realm of knowledge or acquiring and perfecting new skills. Although testing and recording may be made more interesting by adopting varied techniques, they must unavoidably deal with data which has lost its freshness. In consequence it is probably wise to spend only a third or less of the total teaching-time on this form of activity. Similar considerations apply to the kind of homework which involves only learning and memorizing, the success of which can only be assessed by testing in part or all of a classroom period. This is not the best use of classroom time, which should be regarded as a valuable commodity in short supply, to be utilized always in the most effective way possible.

# 15

## Keeping on the Crest of the Wave

MAN is a restless creature everlastingly attempting to modify his environment and adjust himself to it, and since the geography taught in school emphasizes the human aspect much of its data changes. In part this explains the appeal of the subject to the pupil and the heavy demands it places on the conscientious teacher. The successful geography teacher must keep up to date. The specialist, with his firm foundation of geographical knowledge, can easily graft new information on to the old, placing recent events and trends in their correct geographical setting. In addition he knows where he can secure additional relevant material. The general class teacher is in a less favourable position, for his grounding in the subject may be less firm and he has to satisfy the demands made on him by several subjects. The thoughtful person acquires considerable knowledge of current affairs from general reading and from the radio and television, but it may be helpful to mention a few of the chief sources of information of a geographical nature which is topical in character.

Some of the great national newspapers frequently contain up-to-date articles and reports on items of geographical significance. *The Times* is particularly valuable in this respect, providing accurate accounts, well illustrated by maps and pictures. Weekly and monthly periodicals, even the more popular, illustrated examples, often have suitable material, and the geographical magazines, especially the British and American, contain very good pictures and useful articles. The quarterly publication of the Geographical Association, *Geography*, contains a regular feature called "This Changing World," which consists of brief accounts by experts on recent developments in various parts of the world. The American Geographical Society publishes ten times a year an inexpensive broadsheet called *Focus*, each issue of which deals with one country or topic and provides authentic, topical material well illustrated by specially drawn maps. *Keesing's Contemporary Archives* often has material of considerable geographical significance, illustrated with clear maps, and easily found with the aid of the comprehensive index. Current statistics can, of course, be secured from *Whitaker's Almanack*, *The Statesman's Year-book*, and the publications of the United Nations Organizations.

There are other sources, too, which the vigilant teacher will be aware of and utilize. Some find that modern travel books provide much valuable local colour to add the necessary realism in lessons, while others are adept at the introduction of the occasional "newspaper" lesson, which is based on events recently reported in the daily Press, and which can serve to bring out geographical principles. The fresh eruption of a Mediterranean volcano, the bursting of the Mississippi levees, the completion of a new barrage for an Australian irrigation-and-power scheme, or the discovery of a new deposit of uranium, are examples of topics which might arise. Without this alertness and flexibility the geography teacher is in danger of repeating the same material year after year, relying, as it were, on a basic stock-in-trade which can become shop-soiled and drab.

Apart from the increased interest and heightened sense of reality brought to the pupils by this attention to current affairs, there is its equally important bearing on the accuracy of the subject-matter. Textbooks, advanced or elementary,

Southern Limit of Selva

The Tropical Forest
area as usually depicted

Scale: 1:32,000,000

The Forest Area in 1950
[The rest had been felled]

Fig. 15. THE TROPICAL FOREST IN SOUTH-EASTERN BRAZIL

admirable as they may be, soon get out of date in some respects, and if they are followed slavishly, uncorrected by the teacher, they may be responsible for perpetuating error which may persist for a very long time. In fact, some textbooks still to be seen in use are of historical interest rather than geographical value. Pupils are still stating in public examinations that the Amazon Basin is one of the chief producers of raw rubber, that Virginia is the chief tobacco-growing state of North America, that Bendigo is a gold-mining town of significance, that Cornwall produces much tin, that São Paulo grows only coffee (and that most of this is ground up and put into tins of a certain proprietary brand on the spot!), that a part of South Africa is called "German South-west Africa," and that the Indian Sub-continent is still the province of only one state.

Error is also perpetuated by the use of antiquated maps, in the atlas or displayed on the wall, particularly when they show distributions which can be modified by human activity. The maps in Figure 15 provide a striking example. A much-used series of wall maps shows the distribution of forest in Brazil as in the first map whereas, because of the rapid destruction of forest during the last thirty years, the true situation is as shown in the second map. All maps depicting natural vegetation should be scrutinized with great care. Atlas maps are on too small a scale for the distribution to be shown with any accuracy, and in many areas human activity has caused widespread modifications. Second-growth forest is generally very different in character from the original cover, and in some parts of the world for which natural vegetation maps are still much in evidence, the cultivation of crops and the planting of pastures have displaced the natural vegetation, especially in the grassland regions of Manitoba and the Ukraine.

By long usage teachers have become tolerant of other mapped distributions which can lead to error, confusion, or misunderstanding when studied by pupils. Most maps show

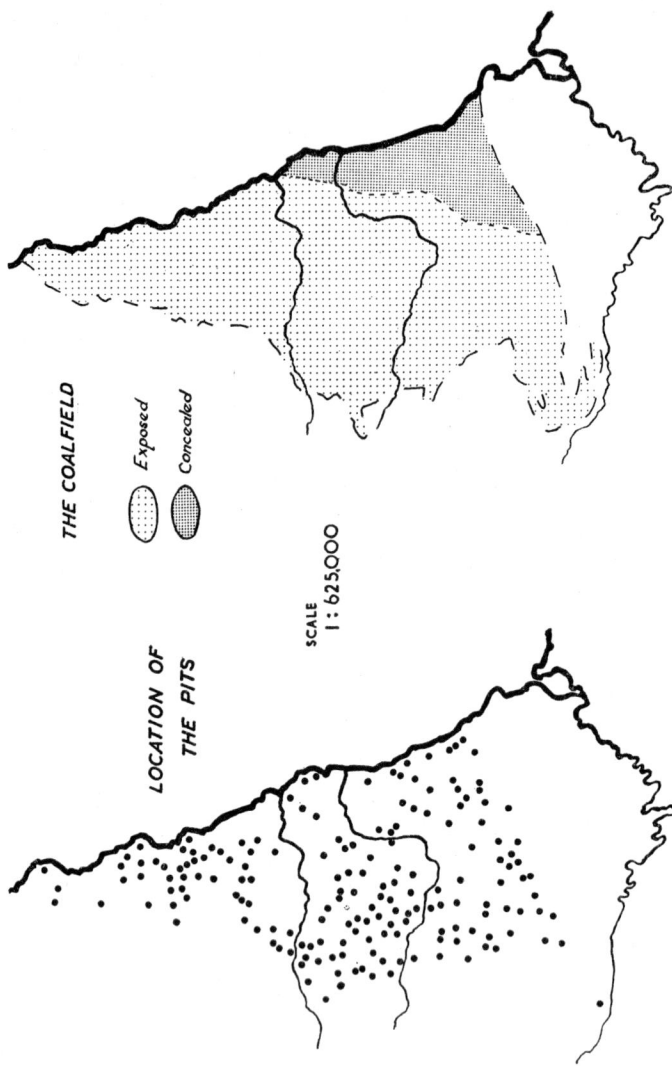

THE COALFIELD

Exposed

Concealed

SCALE
1:625,000

LOCATION OF
THE PITS

Fig. 16. The Northumberland and Durham Coalfield

the distribution of British coalfields by shading or colouring the superficial area of the coal measures, and pupils who have never seen a coalmine get the impression that a coalfield is a continuous stretch of black, dust-besmirched land with innumerable pit headgears, tip heaps, black buildings, and railway lines. Far more valuable and accurate would be a map showing the locations of the pits as in the 1 : 625,000 map of the National Atlas series, for then pupils would be much more ready to appreciate that over most coalfields the widely scattered shafts are separated by considerable areas of normal rural landscape. The two methods of mapping are compared in Figure 16.

Opinions may be divided about the value of using isotherms as indicators of temperature differences. Their limitations and disadvantages are generally fully appreciated, but less critically regarded are population-distribution maps, which show variation by isopleths and layer colouring. These mislead because they give the impression that the considerable area of any one colour has an even density of population, and that the highest density is always some arbitrary and very modest figure, frequently 512 people to the square mile. As already mentioned, this is inaccurate because it hides the very great density which may exist in some large urban areas such as Middlesex or Warwickshire, where the density may be fifty times as great. More use of dot-distribution maps, again as in the National Atlas examples, would give the pupils a more accurate picture of the pattern of population.

Error may be propagated in geography-teaching through the indiscriminate use of generalization, a necessary aid to thought and understanding in certain circumstances for mature, quick minds but less suitable for slower pupils. When generalization is used as a means of simplification it may lead to serious inaccuracy. Examples such as, "cattle-rearing is the chief occupation of the pampas," or "the Spaniards are indolent people," or "most Chinamen live on rice," or to liken the

Asiatic monsoons to gigantic land and sea breezes, are too obvious to need comment, but real danger arises when simplification leads to the suppression of vital facts.

Some textbooks and many teachers repeat, almost without thought, the statement that the Mediterranean type of climate has "rain in winter." Average climatic statistics are readily available and their examination shows that this statement is not the whole truth. The following table gives the mean annual rainfall figures for representative places in various parts of the "Mediterranean" world as they are distributed between the seasons.

RAINFALL IN INCHES

|  | Winter | Spring | Autumn | Summer | Total |
|---|---|---|---|---|---|
| MURCIA | $4\frac{1}{4}$ | $4\frac{1}{2}$ | $5\frac{1}{2}$ | $1\frac{1}{4}$ | 15·1 |
| NAPLES | $10\frac{3}{4}$ | $7\frac{1}{2}$ | $11\frac{3}{4}$ | $2\frac{3}{4}$ | 32·8 |
| CAPE TOWN | $4\frac{3}{4}$ | $11\frac{1}{4}$ | $6\frac{3}{4}$ | 2 | 24·8 |
| ADELAIDE | 8 | $6\frac{3}{4}$ | $4\frac{1}{2}$ | $2\frac{1}{4}$ | 20·6 |
| PERTH | $19\frac{1}{2}$ | $6\frac{1}{2}$ | $7\frac{1}{2}$ | $1\frac{1}{4}$ | 34·8 |

In each case a considerable proportion of the total rainfall occurs in the spring and autumn, and at Murcia and Cape Town the amounts in winter are less than in the other two cool seasons. Other examples would show the same characteristic and help to demonstrate that the safest short statements on the rainfall regime are, "Rain falls in the cool seasons" and, "The summers are dry."

A further point in the consideration of climate may be mentioned. Striving to stimulate thought on the part of the pupils, teachers sometimes describe the climatic characteristics of a region and then invite the pupils to state the crops which are grown there. Since the cultivation of particular crops depends on many factors, not only on climate, this is really asking pupils to guess the answer. It is much sounder, educationally and geographically, if the teacher describes the climate and states the crops, and then asks the pupils to make the deductions about the relationship between the two. The type of questioning which encourages the guessing of facts is a characteristic of the novice and is common in students under training.

Serious error may arise from the attempt to apply a simple, tidy, general explanation to a particular case—for example, the desert of Atacama is sometimes explained as the direct result of the position of the region to the immediate west of the lofty Andes, which shield the coastal strip from the rain-bearing south-east trade winds. The truth is that in the Atacama region winds from the sea are more frequent than winds from the south-east, but they bring no rain because they are sharply cooled in crossing the cold waters of the Humboldt Current. This is not difficult to teach but it takes longer. The teacher must seek to gain relief from the pressure of the over-loaded syllabus whenever he can, but it would be a serious reproach against the integrity of the teaching if it were gained at the expense of accuracy. Examples on these lines could be multiplied. The drought of "Mediterranean" summers is some-times explained as being due to the rainlessness of the trade winds after they have crossed land masses. This ignores the nature of the winds and misrepresents the latitudes where they are most evident. Pupils are sometimes led to believe that the ruggedness of the west coast of Scotland is the result of the battering it receives from Atlantic rollers, while others some-times state that the mildness of the same region is due to the "Gulf Stream."

The teacher's vocabulary can be a source of error and mis-conception. Metaphorical terms, freely used and clearly under-stood by adults, can mislead pupils who hear them for the first time. An expression such as "river basin" obviously needs careful defining, otherwise some pupils may form a concept of the only basin they know—a kitchen utensil. "Belt," "cove," "peak," "(north) pole," and "relief" are other examples, but in the main geographical terms are so beautifully descriptive that to the pupil with a little careful grounding they appear almost self-evident. Of course every teacher would explain a new technical term and proceed slowly enough to ensure that pupils can follow the description of new features. A reasonably intelligent pupil once stated that an Argentine windpump was, "A pump to pump the wind"! Some descriptive phrases need to be used with care. Ireland as "a saucer-shaped island" may be interpreted too literally, and the Pennines as "the backbone of England" has little to commend it. Care must be taken that pupils are clear about the connotation of "grass" when it is applied to savanna or pampas, otherwise English grass of meadow or downland will form the image. The pupils themselves should be led by example to use descriptive phrases with care and accuracy, especially when they write or talk of climatic conditions in foreign lands. With British weather as the standard it is obviously misleading to speak of "winter" in the West Indies or along the Congo, while "very wet" to the London child would be small measure for the summer rain of Bombay or Valdivia. Even bright, mature pupils often incompletely comprehend an idea when it is presented to them for the first time. The candidate who wrote, "The chief occupation of the people of Switzerland is the taking in of tourists; this is an example of an invisible export," was obviously labouring to express an idea only partially understood. Another, answering a question on coastal form, probably had no canine association but much vagueness in mind when he wrote, "There is a little dalmatian along the coast"!

Geography does not attempt to provide an explanation of all distributions and relationships; factors which are present and relevant rarely bear elevation in status to controlling agents. The oft-quoted example of the dampness of the South Lancashire atmosphere and its effect on the location of the cotton industry is a case in point. Sometimes the impression is given that the industry was set up in Lancashire *because* the atmosphere was damp. No doubt this advantage helped to establish and maintain the industry there in face of competition from other regions, but there were other reasons, many of them not geographical, for the initial introduction of cotton. In the same connexion it is often stated that the situation of Liverpool near by, on the west coast and facing America was an important factor in the early days of the industry, but at first all raw cotton came from India and Egypt, and other ports were more favourably placed.

History, politics, economics, and sentiment may all provide more satisfactory and accurate explanations than geography for the particular location of a town, the course of a parish boundary, or the presence of an industry. Geography has a most pervasive influence, and it is right that pupils should have demonstrated to them simple cases of cause and effect in the subject, but older pupils should be aware too, that sometimes other forces or factors may be equally influential.

# 16

## Working with Other Subjects

GEOGRAPHY as a university subject came late into the curriculum partly because its entry was opposed by the older disciplines who despised it as a loose agglomeration of miscellaneous information without clear principles. It is true that geography is a many-faceted subject which makes use of other branches of knowledge, especially geology, mathematics, physics, chemistry, biology, economics, and history, but the modern study has become a philosophy and a discipline which now permits it to rank with older university studies. By its special nature geography acts as a synthesis, combining into a new body elements from many different, but related, sources.

The many-sided nature of the subject, its concentration on reality, its concern with current affairs, in part explain its appeal for pupils in school and the heavy demands it makes on the conscientious teacher. The pivotal nature of geography has encouraged some educationists and geographers to make it the central subject of the curriculum. A notable experiment on these lines was attempted at Ruabon Grammar School and described in 1924.[1] After years of progressive teaching of geography there it became apparent that further progress for many pupils was dependent on their knowledge of other related subjects, and this led eventually to "the entire redraft-

[1] *The Experiment in Geography Teaching at Ruabon County School* (H.M.S.O., 1924).

ing of the geography course in order that the maximum of correlation with other school studies might be obtained." In effect special care was given, especially in science, mathematics, and history, but also in classics, modern languages, and English, to teach these subjects in relation to the requirements of the geography. Thus in mathematics the upper classes gave special attention to gradients, the measurements of heights, and simple map projections; in English and French the set books were often descriptive of travel or topography—for example, Bates's *Naturalist on the Amazons* or Chateaubriand's *Voyage en Amerique*. In Latin special attention was given to Caesar's *Gallic War* relative to descriptions of early Britain; in chemistry emphasis fell on hardness of water, silica, liquefaction, and crystallization, and so on. In history close correlation was not found to be feasible but frequent cross-reference was made in specific topics.

Although this scheme has some attractive features, few geographers (and fewer head teachers) would wish to-day to go as far. Rather similar ideas were responsible for experiments in "Social Studies," which had a meteoric passage across the educational horizon in recent years. Advocates of Social Studies desired the merging of geography, history, economics, and local studies into a new synthesis which had no cognizance of the separate subjects. They based their case on the sound statement that all knowledge is one and indivisible, but rashly concluded that division into subjects was unnecessary, and that pupils should be taught by pursuing "topics," wherever they would lead. Theoretically this looked attractive, but the scheme ignored two important practical difficulties: that only very exceptional teachers could cope with the exceedingly wide range of knowledge needed for the development of any topic, and that this manner of approach soon results in the pupil losing his way in the devious ramifications into which continued subdivision of the topic lead. The directives, the sustaining discipline, and the logical approach of the normal subjects are lacking. Moreover, children are not worried by the presence of "subjects" on the timetable, they like to experience that rather intangible "aura" which each subject develops, and they find the changes of matter, and perhaps of teacher, refreshing, and the educational diet more digestible.

Social Studies, then, is not the best solution. Geography, by its nature, is a subject which can be made to appeal to pupils of all ages and of all standards of ability. It engenders its own way of thought and employs special techniques, although many of the facts employed may lie within the province of other subjects. The good geography teacher is well aware of this, and makes full use of the aspects which are relevant to his geographical theme; he uses them to stress relationships and provide adequate explanation, but he will not pursue them.

A few examples may serve to clarify this point. It has been truly said that, "History without geography is a plant without environment, geography without history is a plant without roots." The sensible geographer frequently uses historical facts in order to make his topic complete and satisfying, and he does so without usurping the work of the history teacher. When considering the growth of a city such as London history and geography are complementary. The early water supply was derived from wells sunk to the clay through the thin gravel cap which provided a well-drained site above flood level. The line of the Roman Walls, in part, followed the banks of small tributaries to the Thames, one of which, the Fleet, or Holbourne, figures much in London's history. History and geography are often intimately linked in the names of many of its streets and squares, and the history of its early boroughs shows the influence exerted over extension by the presence of the London Clay.

Newcastle is an excellent example of a town which grew up at a defended river crossing, and the full story of its significance cannot be brought out without reference to the Roman occupation, the Wall, and the situation of the "new" castle built in the twelfth century, and later the events of the Industrial Revolution linked with the development of the coalfield and the port. Aspects of the geography of parts of Africa might well be linked with a little of the history of its exploration, while the history of the growth of the Russian State during the Christian Era shows close relationship with its geography. The proximity and alignment of such rivers as the Neva, the Volkhov, the West Dvina, and the Dnepr, and their use by early traders between Scandinavia and Constantinople, the presence of easy portages between the rivers, the dense forest which sheltered the early settlements, the passage way of the Volga, the open grasslands to the south allowing entry for the hordes of Genghis Khan and later expansion by the Russians eastward, merely adumbrate the salient features. (Figure 17.) Conversely the good history teacher repeatedly makes use of geography.

With a class which has a sufficient knowledge of chemistry the description of limestone scenery will be incomplete without mention of the action of acidulated water on calcium carbonate and perhaps use of a simple equation; similarly the process of smelting iron ore may be shown to be not a simple melting of the ore but an example of reduction. When considering the growth of crops and the factors which determine soil fertility it may be necessary to mention briefly the nitrogen cycle or the nature and ramifications of the root system of a plant. Geography and geology are obviously closely connected, and there must be much utilization of material which the purist might consider within the province of the latter science —for example, the manner of formation of sand or clay or Moh's scale of hardness. The fact that fish survive in regions of harsh winter where the water of rivers and lakes is frozen to considerable depth calls for reference to the experiment which demonstrates that the water attains its highest density at a temperature of $4°$ C.

In arithmetic ideas of ratio will be involved when scales

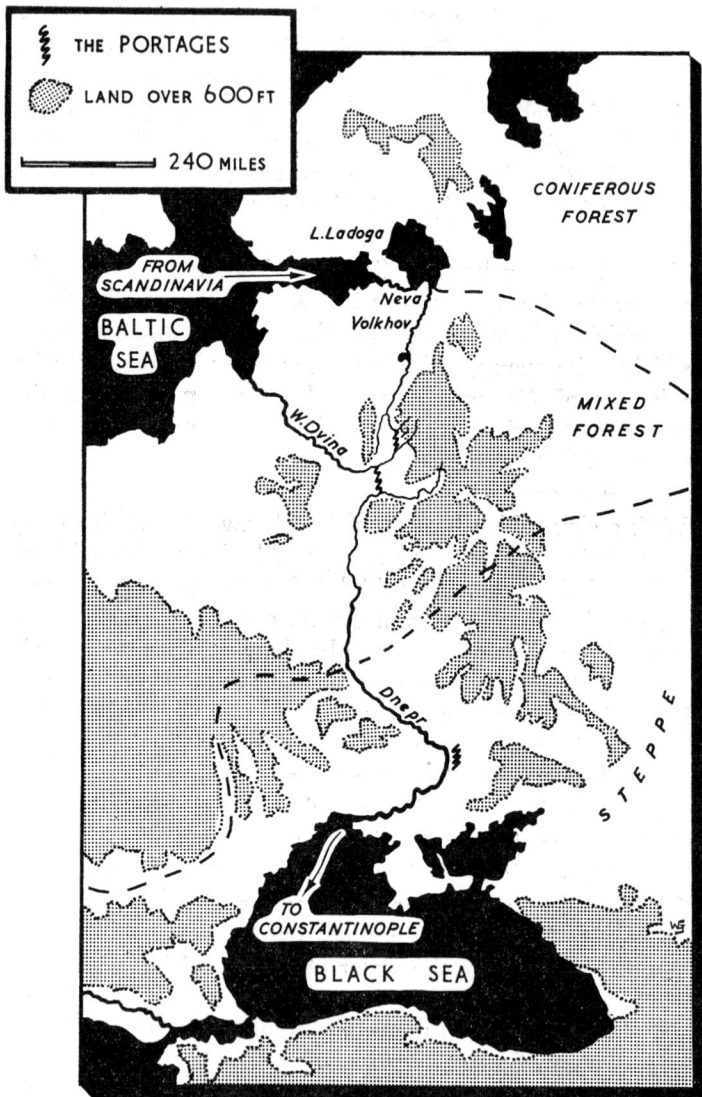

Fig. 17. AN EARLY TRADE ROUTE IN RUSSIA

of maps are under discussion; the relationship between rain-gauge and the corresponding measuring cylinder uses knowledge of the volume of a cylinder and ability to solve simple equations. Discussion of Ordnance Survey map symbols may require the simple geometry of the triangle to explain the purpose of "Trigonometrical Stations."

The artistic display of material in an exhibition or of data on a map suggests co-operation with the art department, the making of models will gain much from the craft teacher's aid, the identification of trees and plants may need the assistance of the biologist. Treatment of the modern geography of Palestine will be the richer if comparison is made with Biblical times, especially in showing how the relief features and the arid, Mediterranean type of climate imposed limits on intensive land utilization.

All this suggests that not only must the geography teacher be ready to use material which lies within the provinces of other subjects, but also that he must be ready to co-operate to the full with other specialists. The wise head teacher makes this easy for his staff by encouraging conferences and discussions and by ensuring that syllabuses in all subjects are available for all members of the staff to see. In many schools a kind of "closed shop" principle seems to be in operation under the influence of which each teacher ploughs his lonely educational furrow irrespective of what his colleagues are doing.

Informal and incidental discussion in the common-room may often help more than planned conferences to secure the friendly co-ordination between subjects which can unify a staff and immeasurably benefit the pupils. Flexible syllabuses may permit the introduction of a topic through the co-operation of a colleague, just when it will be most effective. If the science teacher is able to talk about solutions and suspensions a short time before the geographer wishes to consider the work of running water in modifying the earth's surface, the latter's lessons are going to be much more effective. When the history specialist wishes to consider the distribution of settlements and routes in pre-Roman Britain with a particular class the subject will be understood much better if the geographer has already discussed the contrasting early vegetation on argillaceous and calcareous deposits in this country. Examples could be multiplied and the benefits are obvious, but many serving teachers will scoff at the idea and condemn it as visionary and unrealistic. The fact remains that some staffs are attempting more co-ordination of their work, and the improvement in the effectiveness of lessons has been very marked.

Co-operation between geography and other subjects is particularly natural in the less formal work outside the classroom, especially in connexion with the day excursion for field-work, the school journey, or the school camp. The geographer's consideration of the building materials in the old parish church leads naturally into the historian's emphasis on the shape of the windows or the significance of empty niches. The visit to the local factory may be primarily of geographical importance but it will be enriched by the different aspects which other specialists would emphasize. The geographer may stress the transport and source of the raw material and the distribution of the workers' homes, the science specialist may be able to point out an interesting application of the principle of the wheel and axle or the action of a solvent, and the hygiene teacher may draw attention to methods of reducing muscular fatigue. On these lines the visit becomes a much richer and more worth-while activity.

The argument does not need labouring; co-operation between individuals, among groups of people, and between nations is constantly stressed as a necessary concomitant of progress. It might well find a place in all school staff-rooms.

# I7

## Geography in a New Age

IN a sense the previous chapters have examined aspects of the teaching of geography as they apply to the classrooms and the teachers of to-day. It may be that something more should be said concerning the part that geography can play in the immediate future. It is a platitude to say that we live in times of rapid change, times when the tempo of change is much greater than at any period in history. Scientific and technological developments have achieved revolutions in travel, in oral and visual communication, in synthetic substitutes for natural substances, in the harnessing of nuclear power, and in capacities for human and material destruction.

The advent of the scientific age has emphasized the need for increased numbers of suitably trained men and women, and considerable amendments in educational facilities are being made to meet this need. But the demands of a changing world require adjustments in the outlook and content of all work done in school, not least in geography. What are the new factors which suggest that some reorientation and some re-thinking may be desirable in education generally?

The increased tempo of life shows not only in the speed with which news is transmitted by telephone and radio but also, more important, the rapidity with which ideas may be pro-pagated. The printed word is losing its power as a means for the dissemination of ideas and its place is being taken by visual media. The cinema and television are the new vehicles for exporting culture and defining standards of value as well as for conveying information and instruction. Their function is pervasive and all-embracing because they ignore the barriers of language and thereby take a step towards unifying the world.

The increasing interdependence of the nations of the earth is seen in the increasing transfer of a widening range of raw materials. No country to-day, not even the richly endowed United States or the Soviet Union, is self-sufficient. Britain can survive only at the price of heavy imports of food and raw materials. At the end of 1956 transport in Western Europe was restricted or disrupted for weeks through the cessation of supplies of petroleum from the Middle East, which produces only about 15 per cent. of the world output.

The rapid advance in nuclear physics brings with it threats to the well-being of the whole world. Apart from the inconceivable folly associated with atomic warfare, the carrying out of nuclear tests seems to produce results which can have deleterious effects on peoples and organisms far removed from the test site. The radio-active content of the ice laid down in a Swiss glacier in the year of Hiroshima is higher than that for preceding and succeeding years.

Increasingly man is learning to co-operate all over the world. National boundaries have little significance in the operation of the Postal Union or the Meteorological Service or in the little publicized activities of branches of the United Nations Organization such as the International Labour Office or the Food and Agriculture Organization. Through voluntary effort as well as through the United Nations great strides have been made in the control of the most international visitation —disease. Epidemics can usually be restricted to their sources, infant mortality has been greatly reduced everywhere, and in India during the first half of this century the expectation of life for a man has been increased by thirteen years.

Professor A. L. Banks can now say, "Within a reasonable period I believe that the means of controlling disease, and the ways of promoting health, will be universally applied."[1]

For most people the truth of the shrinking earth is brought home most vividly in the development of astro-nautics and the speed and safety of air transport. In 1919 Alcock and Brown flew the first plane across the Atlantic; to-day, only thirty-eight years later, eighty-four commercial planes cross the same ocean every day. More visitors now enter New York by air than by sea, and before long aircraft weighing as much as the first *Mayflower* will be crossing the Atlantic. London is now one of the greatest passenger ports in the world, and from it New Zealand is only forty flying hours away. Increasing numbers of our pupils have travelled by aeroplane. The launching of earth satellites brings inter-planetary travel within the bounds of possibility.

Facts like these could be multiplied, and they demonstrate that we have entered a new era in which a narrow, nationalistic outlook must give way to global concepts. As Professor David Linton told the Geographical Association in January 1957, "Mankind must be made more aware of the world it lives in, its rigorous limitations and its limited possibilities. Above all it must be assisted and persuaded to think of the world as a whole."[2] To-day technological and scientific development are taking place at an unprecedented speed, increasing man's knowledge of the earth and causing modification in his environment, and since these aspects lie at the heart of all geographical study, the geography teacher must consider actively and immediately what steps he should take to prepare the present generations of pupils for their new responsibilities as citizens of the world as well as of a nation. Attempts might be made on a threefold task :

[1] *Geography*, Vol. XLI, p. 157 (July 1956).
[2] *Geography*, Vol. XLII, p. 22 (January 1957).

(1) To ensure that pupils leave school appreciating and understanding ideas and facts about the geography of the earth as a whole.

(2) To see that they have had opportunities to think about and discuss the geographical problems involved in a global outlook—the "rigorous limitations and the limited possibilities" which the earth imposes upon mankind.

(3) To ensure that pupils leave school aware of the pitfalls associated with the popular dissemination of information and ideas, and know where they can secure accurate facts.

This gives rather a different slant to the geography we teach, particularly, perhaps, in the last year of the secondary course. It is "applied geography," geography for use, the geography which we hope will be employed by pupils for better understanding of the modern world and the part they are to play in it.[1]

If this is so then consideration must be given to the content of the geography to be taught and the method of teaching it. Some years ago M. C. Nokes in his book *Science in Education* was courageous enough to suggest that there were five fundamental aspects of science which every educated person in the country ought to know something about. Similarly, may we venture to suggest that every citizen should be sufficiently educated geographically to understand something of the following five aspects :

(1) The distribution and growth of the population of the world

(2) World food resources, standards of nutrition in different regions, and the geographical aspects of disease

(3) The distribution, exploitation, and transport of raw materials

[1] See also "Geography and the Development of World Understanding" (R. C. Honeybone), *Handbook for Geography Teachers*, p. 55.

   (4) Power resources, present and potential
   (5) World transport systems and their relationship with the
       British Isles

Such a list may shock the academic geographer for it contains no mention of the basic aspects of the subject such as geomorphology, climatology, and the regional concept. But in proposing these aspects there is no suggestion that the fundamentals as expressed in the foregoing chapters be neglected, rather that they will be brought out all the more strongly by being *applied*.

By way of example let us consider the geographical background to the problems which underlie Egyptian economy. As already advocated, we start from the human angle—the Egyptian peasant, what he is like, and the kind of work he does. Then we should note that there are twenty-two million people in Egypt, which gives a density of 1500 a square mile (twice the average for England and Wales). The amount of cultivated land per head of the population is 0·28 acres—about three times the size of an average allotment in this country. Egypt has few resources other than the land and the labour of the people, and, while the sale of the chief commercial crop —cotton—permits purchase of some foreign wheat, most of the country's subsistence depends on homegrown food. The average daily consumption of food per head amounts to 2340 calories, which is fifty calories below what dieticians consider a basic minimum for those climatic conditions. The people therefore are undernourished, and the situation worsens progressively because the population increases by half a million every year. The essential need, therefore, is for more food either from at home, which means more land under cultivation as well as better yields from the existing crop-land, or from abroad. Here the normal features of Egyptian geography, its structure and relief, the soil and hydrology, the climate, are relevant. More cultivated land waits on more

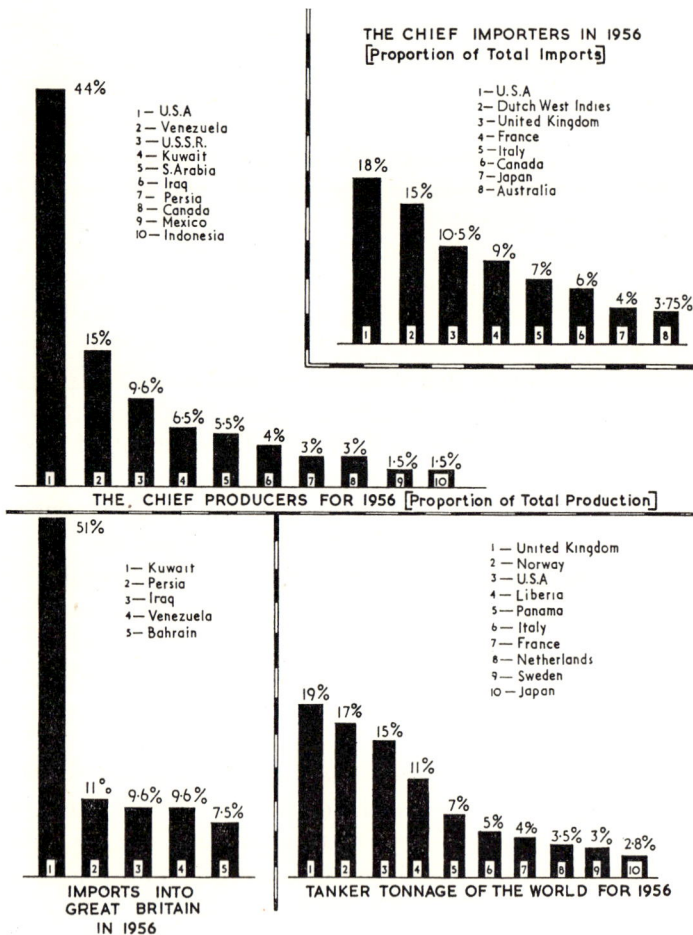

THE CHIEF IMPORTERS IN 1956
[Proportion of Total Imports]

1 — U.S.A
2 — Dutch West Indies
3 — United Kingdom
4 — France
5 — Italy
6 — Canada
7 — Japan
8 — Australia

1 — U.S.A
2 — Venezuela
3 — U.S.S.R.
4 — Kuwait
5 — S.Arabia
6 — Iraq
7 — Persia
8 — Canada
9 — Mexico
10 — Indonesia

THE CHIEF PRODUCERS FOR 1956 [Proportion of Total Production]

1 — Kuwait
2 — Persia
3 — Iraq
4 — Venezuela
5 — Bahrain

1 — United Kingdom
2 — Norway
3 — U.S.A
4 — Liberia
5 — Panama
6 — Italy
7 — France
8 — Netherlands
9 — Sweden
10 — Japan

IMPORTS INTO
GREAT BRITAIN
IN 1956

TANKER TONNAGE OF THE WORLD FOR 1956

Fig. 18. SOME FACTS ABOUT PETROLEUM

water for irrigation, additional control of the Nile, and improved methods. Here is regional geography but with a new slant which stresses the world relationships of the region.

"Resources" geography has long been a feature of school courses, but in the new approach it would be treated from a global and not a regional viewpoint. Suppose the subject were "petroleum." The aspects which could receive attention might be the *relative* significance of the chief producers shown graphically (Figure 18), the situations and geographical features of the producing areas, the requirements of consumers and the chief importers the means of transport by land and sea, oil-refining, industrialization, standards of living, other sources of power. Much variation is possible here, but the aim would be to present a world picture, not a regional one.

The aspect of global geography which calls most obviously for inclusion is "Air Transport," a very big subject which cannot be fully considered here. For purposes of illustration let us take two facets of the topic:

(1) The Location of Airports
(2) The Orientation of Routes

Features which might be included are:

### (1) *The Location of Airports*

The nature of the terrain, size of airfield relative to the type of aircraft, situation with regard to great cities (it takes longer to travel from Central London to the airport than to fly to Paris), climatic aspects, altitude and atmospheric pressure relative to length of runway, sources of fuel, contributing means of transport, etc.

### (2) *The Orientation of Routes*

The air has no frontiers, the troposphere and stratosphere, purpose (freight and passengers), limitations, choice of routes, great circle routes, intermediate land/sea surface, meteorology, etc.

The second example is of importance because it brings again to the fore the need to employ the globe and not the atlas map, in the classroom. It emphasizes too the changed significance of some parts of the earth. The North Pole lies on the direct route from Copenhagen to Tokyo, the Arctic Ocean has become a new "mediterranean" sea, and obscure islands like Wake and the Cocos Islands have become important as intermediate landing-places.

Many other specialized uses of aircraft illustrate both the geographical and global aspects of this topic : in exploration—internationally organized as in Antarctica or less spectacularly in Canada—for topographical and land-use surveying through highly developed aerial photography, for the mapping of geology and prospecting by gravimetric and radio-active methods, for soil surveys as in Mesopotamia, for farming by dusting with insecticides, etc., and in forestry for fire-fighting.

Having in mind the new concepts, the teaching of the geography of the British Isles might need some modification and reorientation. It may be desirable to give less attention to the regional aspects of the subject and more to the position of the country with regard to the import of raw materials, the relative significance of home-produced and foreign food supplies, Britain's place in the world as a manufacturing nation (and, incidentally, whether she has any advantages apart from the skill of her people and the capacity to work), world transport routes and Britain's connexion with them, and Britain's relationships with Commonwealth countries, Western Europe, and the United States. The globe will again take precedence as a teaching aid as the significance of the British Isles as the western outpost of the "World Island" of Eurasia and near the centre of the land hemisphere of the world is emphasized.

These suggestions at once provoke the questions, "How are

we to do all this?" and "Where is the time to come from?"
Some indication has already been given as to method; in
regional geography it is really only the slant which is different.
A normal lesson on Northern China might begin with a
sample study on a typical farmer near Peking and describe his
work through the seasons, the crops he grows, method of
irrigation, the relationship of his work to the soil, drainage
and climate, his farmhouse, etc. The new aspect could be
introduced by mentioning the tiny size of the farm, which
results from the large population of China and the pressure
on the land, and the resulting low standards of nutrition.
These are the aspects which have global significance. If the
lesson takes the form of a comparison between conditions in
North and South China the work can easily be oriented to
include these fundamental facts. Or, as was suggested in
Chapters 9 and 10, pupils may be led to make fundamental
discoveries for themselves by giving them data (or letting them
look it up) such as total population, total area of cultivated
land, rate of increase of the population, production of main
food-crops, consumption per head, expectation of life, etc.,
and the facts shown in diagrams. Even if the pupils do not
make them they are useful and effective teaching aids (Figure
19) made by the teacher. It might be mentioned too that some
of the topics touched on above could fit in admirably in the
concentric scheme described in Chapter 13.

The problem of time is always with us. In this connexion it
seems that the needs of two groups should be differentiated—
those who are not concerned with an external examination
and those who are. The first group may be less well endowed
intellectually and they may be slower, but they will grow up
into sensible, reasonable citizens, forming more than half of
the next generation. The absence of the shackles of an external
examination presents an opportunity which should be made
the most of. Particularly in the last year of the course the
pupils have got to see some purpose in school work, they need

| CHINA | U.S.A. |
|---|---|

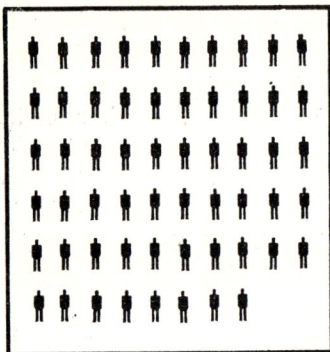 

AREA 3·76 MILLION SQ. MILES    AREA 3·0 MILLION SQ. MILES
POPULATION 583 MILLION    POPULATION 162·4 MILLION

·58 ACRES    2·94 ACRES

CULTIVATED LAND PER HEAD

AVERAGE CALORIES PER HEAD PER DAY

| 2030 | 3120 |
|---|---|

Fig. 19. COMPARATIVE DIAGRAMS

to see it related to the lives they are looking forward to living when they leave school. It is suggested that much of what has been outlined above is the sort of material which can stimulate interest in both boys and girls, especially if discussion can be encouraged and thought stimulated. If this is done then probably it would be wise to substitute for the normal syllabus of the last year some of the aspects outlined above.

To an increasing degree, the later part of the course followed by many boys and girls, particularly those who remain at school beyond the age of fifteen, includes some "special study," usually of a vocational kind, such as engineering or commerce, catering or building. This is likely to be true of still more pupils when the school-leaving age is raised to sixteen. Among the pupils at present concerned, some may have an examination objective while others may not. The vocational interest gives vitality to the whole course, if well used, and the geography teacher is in a particularly good position to make his special contribution especially if he stresses the "global" aspects. All technical subjects have important geographical aspects, and it is vital that future engineers, for example, should have a good background knowledge of the needs and character of the industry which they wish to enter. Much of this background is geographical, and for such pupils the later part of the geography course, while remaining true geography, ought to be slanted towards the field of employment which the pupil expects to enter, and which determines his "special study" while still at school.

The problem is more difficult for the examination group but it is not insuperable. Within any set syllabus, as every good teacher knows, there is room for much incidental teaching, teaching "on the side," which often has significance far beyond the time spent on it; in fact it often does more good than material right on the syllabus because it stimulates interest and thought. As suggested above, it should be quite possible to introduce into the normal regional work aspects which are also of global importance. One other point may be made. The examination system was designed to be the servant, not the master, of the schools, and the examining bodies are always ready to modify syllabuses if there is a demand for change. Also, in order not to stereotype the work of schools, the examining bodies agreed to let schools submit their individual syllabuses. The significant thing is that very few schools do so.

Underlying the views expressed in these pages has run the conception that geography is a worth-while subject pre-eminently suited as a medium of real education for girls and boys of all ages and abilities. It is flexible, and adaptable to changing needs, and, resting on a basis of sound principles, it can provide a vehicle for the exercise of logical thought. Above all the subject provides a valuable body of knowledge which, well taught, can interest the pupil and prepare him to become a responsible citizen in a rapidly changing world.

The world to-day has become so complex, and events follow one another with such bewildering rapidity, that the ordinary person tends to withdraw, and takes the negative attitude that the professionals, the politicians, the scientists can look after things. It cannot be stressed too strongly that all modern developments are the result of human effort, and that man *is* master of his fate if only he will not abdicate from his respon-sibilities. Every individual should realize that in one way or another, he can exert some influence on the course of events for good or ill, and the geography teacher is in a favourable position to disseminate this important concept.

As in all discussion of educational topics, here we are brought back to the fundamental aspect—it all depends on the teacher. The quality of education in this country depends not chiefly on equipment, buildings, or facilities, but on the quality of the individual teachers. Particularly heavy demands are made upon the teacher of geography. He needs to have a firm grasp of the basic principles of the subject and a sound body of knowledge. He needs to be widely read, especially in travel literature, and to be physically active so as to undertake field-work. He has to adopt all possible means to keep himself up to date. Above all he must be a person of wide interests, for much of the success of his teaching depends on his ability to handle material from related subjects and to integrate it and distil it for the benefit of his pupils.

Thus portrayed the geography teacher sounds a paragon. It is a commentary on the high level of much of the geography teaching to-day that there are such people; the knowledge that in many more enthusiasm and interest only wait on guidance and help has provided the stimulus for the writing of this book.

# A Brief Bibliography

BARNARD, H. C. : *Principles and Practice of Geography Teaching* (University Tutorial Press, 1948).

BRIAULT, E. W. H., AND SHAVE, D. W. : *Geography in the Secondary School* (Geographical Association, new ed., 1960).

FAIRGRIEVE, J. : *Geography in School* (University of London Press, 1949).

GARNETT, O. : *Fundamentals in School Geography* (Harrap, 1949).

GOPSILL, G. H. : *The Teaching of Geography* (Macmillan, 1956).

HEATON, P. R. : *The Geography Room in a Secondary School* (Geographical Association, 1955).

I.A.A.M. : *The Teaching of Geography in Secondary Schools* (Philip, new ed., 1952).

LAYTON, E., AND WHITE, J. B. : *The School Looks Around* (Longmans, 1948).

SAXELBY, C. H. (Ed. by) : *A Geographer's Reference Book* (Geographical Association, 1955).

SCOTTISH EDUCATION DEPT. : *Geography in Secondary Schools* (H.M.S.O., 1951).

SIMPSON, C. A. : *The Study of Local Geography* (Methuen, 1950).

THRALLS, Z. A. : *The Teaching of Geography* (Appleton Century Crofts, 1958).

UNESCO : *Towards World Understanding VII:* "Some Suggestions on the Teaching of Geography" (H.M.S.O., 1950).

UNESCO : *Towards World Understanding X:* "A Handbook of Suggestions on the Teaching of Geography" (H.M.S.O., 1951).

UNIVERSITY OF LONDON, INSTITUTE OF EDUCATION: *Handbook for Geography Teachers,* edited by G. J. Cons (Methuen, 1955). (New ed. edited by R. C. Honeybone, 1960.)

WALKER, J.: *Aspects of Geography Teaching in Schools* (Oliver and Boyd, 1953).

WALLIS, B. C.: *The Teaching of Geography* (Cambridge University Press, 1916).

YOUNG, T. U.: *Farm Studies in the Teaching of Geography* (Association of Agriculture, 1959).

# ARTICLES ON ASPECTS OF TEACHING WHICH HAVE APPEARED IN RECENT VOLUMES OF "GEOGRAPHY"

BALCHIN, W. G. V.: "Local Climatic Studies for Schools," Vol. XXXIII, p. 128 (Sept. 1948).

BENNETT, W. J., AND COURTENAY, P. P.: "Teaching Geography in Malaya," Vol XLIII, p. 14 (April 1958).

BOSCOW, H.: "Geography in the Secondary Modern School," Vol. XXXII, p. 13 (March 1947).

BRIAULT, E. W. H.: "The Study of Local Geography as an Integral Part of the School Course," Vol. XXXVIII, p. 29 (Jan. 1953).

BRICE, W. C.: "The Anatolian Village," Vol. XL, p. 461 (July 1955).

BROADHURST, B. M., AND PHILLIPS, R. F.: "The Teaching of Geography for International Understanding," Vol. XXXVI, p. 83 (May 1951).

BROOKS, L.: "Some Thoughts on the Present-day Teaching of Geography in Schools," Vol. XXXVII, p. 63 (April 1952).

BUDDEN, L. C.: "Holiday Geography," Vol. XXXV, p. 192 (Sept. 1950).

COBB, R. T.: "Topographical Maps for Use in the Classroom," Vol. XLI, p. 187 (July 1956).

COLEMAN, A.: "Field-work in Schools: A Sample Traverse in East Kent," Vol. XXXIX, p. 264 (Nov. 1954).

COURSE, E. A.: "Railway Geography in the Secondary Modern School," Vol. XL, p. 40 (Jan. 1955).

FOSTER, R. J.: "Individual Projects in Grammar School Geography," Vol. XXXV, p. 185 (Sept. 1950).

HADDON, J.: "An Experiment in Teaching Geography," Vol. XXXIII, p. 190 (Dec. 1948); "Newspapers in the Geography Class," Vol. XXXVI (May 1951).

HALL, G. S.: "Regional Geography in the Grammar School," Vol. XLIII, p. 259 (Nov. 1958).

HARRIS, H. L.: "An Experiment in Visual Education," Vol. XXXIV, p. 152 (Sept. 1949).

HEAMON, A. J.: "Geography Teaching in the Comprehensive School," Vol. XLIII, p. 244 (Nov. 1957).

HIGGINS, L. S.: "The Geographical Association and Geography in the Secondary Modern School," Vol. XXXII, p. 17 (March 1947).

HONEYBONE, R. C.: "Balance in Geography and Education," Vol. XXXIX, p. 91 (April 1954).

HOWARTH, O. J. R.: "The Commonwealth in the Geography Syllabus," Vol. XXXIX, p. 5 (Jan. 1954).

JAY, L. J.: "Significant Place-names in School Geography," Vol. XXXIX, p. 28 (Jan. 1954); "The Teaching of Geography in the Secondary Schools of France," Vol. XLIII, p. 200 (July 1958).

JONES, P. A.: "Meteorology in Schools," Vol. XXXIX, p. 182 (July 1954).

LAMBERT, A. M.: "Early Maps and Local Studies," Vol. XLI, p. 167 (July 1956).

LEARMONTH, A. T. A. AND A. M.: "Aspects of Village Life in Indo-Pakistan," Vol. XL, p. 145 (July 1955).

LONG, M.: "Children's Reactions to Geography Pictures," Vol. XXXVIII, p. 100 (April 1953).

LYONS, H. R.: "Local Geography and the Five-year Course in a Grammar School," Vol. XXXIV, p. 65 (June 1949).

MILLWARD, R.: "The Place of Travel in the Geography Syllabus," Vol. XXXIII, p. 13 (March 1948).

PRUDDEN, H. C.: "Classroom Work on the Daily Weather Report," Vol. XXXIX, p. 188 (July 1954).

Rees, H. : "Lloyd's List as a Source for Port Study in Schools," Vol. XL, p. 249 (Nov. 1955).

Roberson, B. S. : "Canadian Farms in the Classroom," Vol. XLI, p. 178 (July 1956).

Roberson, B. S., and Long, M. : "Sample Studies—The Development of a Method," Vol. XLI, p. 248 (Nov. 1956).

Scarfe, N. V. : "The Teaching of Geography in Schools," Vol. XXXIV, p. 57 (June 1949).

Sealy, K. R. : "A Review of Some West European Statistical Sources," Vol. XXXIX, p. 192 (July 1954).

Sparrow, G. W. H. : "Geography with Eleven Year Old C Streams," Vol. XXXV, p. 190 (Sept. 1950).

Suggate, L. S. : "Aspects of Geography Teaching in the Grammar School," Vol. XLI, p. 1 (Jan. 1956).

Wilks, H. C. : "A Scheme of Field Work Throughout a School," Part, I, Vol. XLI, p. 15 (Jan. 1956), Part II, Vol. XLI, p. 108 (April 1956).

# Index